Advent/
Christmas

Proclamation 4

Aids for Interpreting
the Lessons of the Church Year

Advent/
Christmas

Gordon W. Lathrop

Series B

FORTRESS PRESS   **MINNEAPOLIS**

PROCLAMATION 4
Aids for Interpreting the Lessons of the Church Year
Series B: Advent/Christmas

Library of Congress Cataloging-in-Publication Data

(Revised for ser. B, vols. 1–4)

Proclamation 4.

Consists of 24 volumes in 3 series designated A, B, and C, which correspond to the cycles of the three year lectionary. Each series contains 8 basic volumes with the following titles: [1] Advent-Christmas, [2] Epiphany, [3] Lent, [4] Holy Week, [5] Easter, [6] Pentecost 1, [7] Pentecost 2, and [8] Pentecost 3. In addition there are four volumes on the lesser festivals.
    By Christopher R. Seitz and others.
    Includes bibliographies.
    1. Bible—Homiletical use.   2. Bible—Liturgical lessons, English.   3. Bible—Criticism, interpretation, etc.   4. Common lectionary.   5. Church year.
I. Seitz, Christopher R.   II. Title: Proclamation four.
BS381.2.S37   1990   264'.34   88-10982
ISBN 0-8006-4169-8 (series B, Advent-Christmas)

The paper used in this publication meets the minimum requirements of American National Standard for Information Sciences—Permanence of Paper for Printed Library Materials, ANSI Z329.48-1984.   ∞ ™

Manufactured in the U.S.A.   AF 1-4169

94   93   92   91   90   1   2   3   4   5   6   7   8   9   10

Contents

Introduction

ORIGIN AND MEANING OF THE CHRISTMAS CYCLE

In the Northern Hemisphere the new year comes in relative darkness. The daylight is at its briefest, and only as January and February move along do we begin to note that the sun has turned, that the solstice has in fact occurred already on December 21. The new year is "born" in that darkness where the sun itself seems to have a new "birth." After all, a year among us is a measure of the cycle of our planet in relationship to the sun. The emotion-laden words "old" and "new" are used to describe the time of dying light and dying vegetation in autumn and the time of darkness yielding to growing light in midwinter.

Such darkness pulls to itself more than customs regarding calendar designations. The darkness of the year's end readily becomes a metaphor for our fears, our failures, our death. And calling the time a "new year" and experiencing the turning of the sun suggest the possibility of hope.

It is no wonder that the time of the sun's turning became a time of feasts. Lights and food and gifts and stories have been set against the darkness, becoming the focus and matrix for communal hopes. The city of Rome (which knows a quite darkened December) had its Saturnalia on December 17 and through the following week. The feast was a celebrative reenactment of a mythic golden age of fruitful abundance, leisure, and equality, interpreted as the presence in the land of the old agricultural gods Saturn and Ops. Then, in A.D. 274, under the influence of new cults of salvation, official Rome adopted its "birthday of the Unconquered Sun" on December 25 (regarded then to be the date of the solstice) as a general feastday for the city and the empire. Such feasts have been found throughout the Northern Hemisphere, East and West. Yule, Divali (a Hindu new year festival), and Hannukah are only a few examples. Each feast has its own pattern of myth, its own history of hopes imaged as lights against the darkness. But interweaving abundance, leisure, and social reversals amidst the threatened privations of winter is a common way to express those hopes. Food when the ground is frozen, abundance in the face of the fear of nothing, light in darkness—such things mark the feasts as "midwinter protests."

Christmas is no exception. Some scholars believe Christmas originated in Rome as a Christianization of the feast of the sun's birth. The earliest

"Advent" may have come about, quite independently of that Roman Christianization, through the insistence of bishops in Spain that gatherings in the church be held as a counterobservance during the time of the Saturnalia and other year-end/year-beginning festivals. That Roman Christians celebrated the solstice would explain why a Christian mosaic, datable to the late third or early fourth century and found in the necropolis excavated under St. Peter's in Rome, depicts Christ as the one driving the heavenly sun-chariot. Indeed, Constantine's heavenly sign may have been the Christ-monogram or it may have been the sun, or, given the evidence of Constantine's ongoing syncretism, it may have been both! The evidence for the Spanish counterobservance is the fourth canon of the council of Saragossa in A.D. 380: "For the twenty-one days beginning with December 17 no one is allowed to be absent from the assembly nor to lie hidden at home." Communal assembly and communal prayer were to balance the private leisure and the private excess of the current cultural feasts of the year's turning. Both Advent and Christmas were ways to show forth Christian faith in the midst of the year-end feasts. Only later were they woven together into a single cycle.

Other scholars propose that Christmas originated in elaborate and symbol-laden calculations of the birthday of Jesus, calculations encouraged by the growth of christological orthodoxy. Influenced by the Jewish expectation that Messiah should come at Passover and by the tradition that the deathdays and the birthdays of the patriarchs coincided, some Christians came to regard Pascha and the conception of Jesus (that is, the crucifixion and the "annunciation") as having occurred on the same day of the year. This date was understood to have been either March 25 or April 6, the date of the spring equinox in different calendars. But then the birth of Christ would have occurred a perfect nine months later, at the winter solstice (December 25 or January 6). Indeed, some of these calculators began their work by placing the annuciation of John the Baptist at the autumn equinox. Zechariah was considered to be busy in the Temple with the rites of the month Tishri—the day of atonement and the feast of tabernacles—when the angel came. The result of this correspondence was that the annunciation of Jesus "in the sixth month" of Elizabeth's pregnancy (Luke 1:26) would be set at the spring equinox, and the birth of the Baptist nine months after conception would occur at the summer solstice. Thus, the annunciation to Mary, the paschal events of Jesus' death and resurrection, and the springtime of the Mediterranean world were all seen to coincide.

Such calculations about the births of John and Jesus in correspondence to the solstices and equinoxes could have been made quite independently of the surrounding culture. The origin of Christian festivals could have had its own internal logic. It seems more likely, however, that the calculations would have been intended to set out biblical and scholarly reflection as an anchor and a transformation of already existent solar pieties. In any case, one ends up with scriptural accounts set next to—stretched on the frame of—the experience of seasonal solar events.

Whether or not such calculations served as the "origin" of the feasts, it seems clear that the various Christian observances that began to be held at the time of the "new year," when juxtaposed to the observances of the surrounding cultures, proposed a new content and meaning for year's end festivals, just as the Christian Pascha had accepted and transformed the ancient Passover. Like the insistence of the Saragossa council that Christians assemble during the festival days of December, the calculations propose a new reality placed by God into the midst of the feasts of spring and of winter. For Christians the "sun" born in our midst is Jesus Christ.

The two theories of the origins of the Christmas cycle need not be opposed to each other. The "Christianization" of the Unconquered Sun and of Saturnalia is a way of speaking of what happened popularly. The calculation theories offer one window into the mind of theologians and bishops and preachers. We do not know which came first.

But we do know that the result has been that Christmas is a remarkable combination of food, leisure, and lights—the ancient festal matrices of midwinter hope—with the Word of God. The cycles of the sun provide a language with which to speak of Christ. That "language" includes the popular events of year's end observance. Christ, present in the world, is our sun in darkness, our eternal "new year," our feast, our light, our rest, our lively connection to each other. This is a language that speaks powerfully to our hearts. But the word of God juxtaposed to this feast provides also a critique of the solar observances that is more than simply old episcopal fear of excess. When the darkness of the year is over, we are still in darkness. When waiting for the feast is over, we are waiting still in the poverty and wretchedness that everywhere cries out for God. And when the Christmas feast is past, the assembly will still gather every Sunday around the burning light of Christ shining forth in the Scriptures and around the table of the Lord, which is always our great festival of eating and drinking in the presence of God.

This critique of the solstice observance makes it possible for Christians to keep the old Christmas cycle in the modern world. The waiting poor join together in Advent expectation at any time of year. Christ our burning sun may be celebrated in the Southern Hemisphere at the summer solstice, the time of the longest daylight, or in the tropics, where the sun's variations are hardly noted. And the one celebrated at year's end draws us inevitably to the beginning and end of all feasts, that "equinox" in which his death and resurrection is the renewal of the world. Christmas is held because of Easter. Christmas points again to Easter. Drawing to the paschal center of our faith is what the old calculations of Christ's birthdate originally meant to do.

THE STRUCTURE OF CHRISTMAS PREACHING AND OF THIS BOOK

It is important for preachers and students of the liturgy of the word in the Christmas cycle to understand, with some sympathy, that Advent and Christmas are solstice observances. Then they may understand that the primary tool in the liturgy for the transformation of these observances—and, thus, the transformation of ourselves—is the setting out of biblical texts within these days of cultural festival. The liturgy brings to full expression the powerful language of darkness and longing for the sun. This liturgy is celebrated in a culture still madly trying to express its hopes at year's end, albeit in the inept and sometimes destructive ways of consumerism. But let the Christians gather in waiting assembly through these December days, underneath and beside this festival. Let the waiting be filled with texts that speak of the sure hope for God's salvation. Then let the principal feast day and day of rest, the old day of the sun's birth, echo with the name of the sun of righteousness and with texts full of his presence.

Biblical texts set next to solstice celebrations are keys to understanding the work of the Christmas cycle preacher. This juxtaposition was the ancient work of the Saragossa council or of the calendrical calculators. It is a way to understand how the two theories of the origin of Christmas may relate to each other—solstice Christianized or Christian texts read as speaking of solstices and equinoxes—that Christ may be proclaimed as salvation for this world. This juxtaposition is still the key to the lively and imaginative work of speaking Christ to the heart.

Biblical texts set next to solstice celebrations are also intended to be the key to the structure of this volume. For each Sunday and feast day, the section "About the Texts" looks exegetically at the appointed pericopes as they are read side-by-side in the assembly, before the table of the Lord. This section looks at *biblical texts* in the Christmas cycle.

The purpose of the assembly is to gather us together by the power of the Spirit into Christ and so into God. Because of this trinitarian purpose, the first lesson with which I deal is the Gospel, our entryway to knowledge of the Trinity in the revelation of Christ. The other texts then enrich the church's proclamation set forth in the Gospel. Series B texts for Advent and Christmas will require of us careful attention to all four Gospels and to the way individual pericopes function within the flow of those Gospels to speak the meaning of Christ.

The First Lesson, from the Hebrew Scriptures, is examined next. Taken seriously, in its own history, this text is also regarded as scripture for Christian assembly and preaching. Indeed, it could be considered the "text" for the "sermon" that is the Gospel. Whereas the Hebrew Scriptures are, as Luther says, the *written* text in a primary sense, the Gospel is always an *oral* event, based on those Scriptures. The written Gospel text simply provides a canon for the ongoing oral event in the "mouth-house" that is the church.

The church gathers around this text and sermon. The Second Lesson provides language for the current gathered assembly to understand itself. Paul and the other epistle writers, addressing congregations, can be heard as providing to us "the horizon of the church" (William Skudlarek).

We study the texts in this order that light may be cast on the different order of the reading in the assembly. There the "text" is read first. Then the church is evoked. Then, in the midst of text and gathering, the gospel is disclosed.

When considering pericopes read in Advent and Christmas, such liturgical exegesis must keep in mind the celebrations of the year's end as the place in which the texts are read. "Around the Texts" briefly presents liturgical characteristics from these celebrations themselves, as partial evocations of what is occurring in the church and in the culture. In order to preach, the preacher must fill out such evocations with a fuller and detailed knowledge of the local liturgy and congregation, of the church's liturgical tradition, and of the events in the culture. It is to be hoped that at the meeting place between the texts and what is around the texts the sermon may arise. This section looks at biblical texts in the *Christian cycle*.

In this volume, the church year is understood to be a remarkable way of holding *our* actual and current life under the light of the Word of God. It is not a "reliving" of the life of Christ. Modern renewal has proposed, for example, that Easter is a Christian way of interpreting Passover today, and that baptisms be done at this Passover, thereby transforming the meaning of springtime with an overlay of biblical and liturgical tradition. Lent, in this perspective, is the time of our baptismal preparation and of our baptismal renewal. By the same standard, Advent and Christmas are not a reenacting of holy history with us pretending to be the ancient waiting messianic Jews and singing happy birthday to the baby. They are, rather, ways of speaking the word of God into the solstice festivals being celebrated today.

In this volume, then, *Advent* is understood as a period of waiting for the sun's turning that has been extended to become a symbol for all human waiting for life and peace. The season is remarkably appropriate to the human condition in all times. Christ's historic presence in our world and his hidden coming now, in the Word, become joyful down payments on the hoped-for manifest day of God. Every Sunday gathering is intended to be such a down payment, such an encounter with Christ. When Sunday occurs in Advent we are taught again that the presence of Christ does not do away with waiting, but that Christ forms us more deeply to wait with the world. This year we will be taught by Mark's Gospel that the eschatological fulfillment itself is a deeper form of waiting.

Christian eschatological language transfigures the time of waiting and festival in the world. When this language is set next to Christmas preparations and Christmas parties, there is always something of the spirit of Saragossa. Not that the world's celebrations are scolded; not much comes of that when the celebrations are themselves such a deep human need and when the church's best pastoral instincts have always been interested in the transformation, not the elimination, of profound human symbolization. But then the gathering in the church is full of silence and waiting set counter to whatever Saturnalias are being celebrated. This silence proposes to carry the energy of that Saturnalia toward a deeper hope for a real golden age for all the earth, rather than a brief celebration for just ourselves imagining a mythic golden age that never was.

Advent has its own integrity as a way to propose Christian faith in December. It is dealt with here as if it were not just preparation for Christmas, not time for pageants and Christmas decorations. Advent in the church is intended as a time to feel the current reality of waiting in the world. Such waiting provides its own language for fully speaking the gospel of Christ, and it provides a realism and honesty that the human heart longs to hear. When Advent is allowed to be its own Christian response to solstice-time, it then also becomes a fine preparation for Christmas.

In this volume *Christmas* is understood as a twelve-day-long feast of the sun's return, made to speak the gospel. The principal images that are used in the liturgy to speak of the mercy that is given in Christ are images of the sun, of light, and of the fruitful land yielding a full table. It is the presence of Christ in this world, not just his birth, that is understood to fulfill the ancient hopes of the solstice feast. The principal Gospel lesson of the feast is John 1:1-18 ("The true light was coming into the world . . . the word became flesh . . . we have beheld his glory"), not the birth narratives.

But the birth narratives are read too, as one form of the beginning of the gospel of our redemption, as signs of the presence of God's promise. They too echo the theme of light. In Matthew there is the star and in Luke the angelic glory and the song of Simeon. But these birth narratives are read especially as bearing within themselves seeds of the mystery of the cross at the spring equinox. In Matthew there is the opposition of Herod and the slaughter of the children; in Luke there is the poverty of the child and the prophecy of rejection. It is the crucified and risen Christ present now who is the sun risen in our darkness and is the table of mercy for all peoples.

Both Advent and Christmas are treasures of the church. They are models of the juxtaposition of the Word of God to human culture and to human hope. And, whether they are celebrated in the extremes of either of the hemispheres or in the tropics, they are meant to proclaim the saving mercy of God for all the earth, for all its peoples, indeed, for the sun and stars and the universe itself.

The First Sunday in Advent

Lutheran	Roman Catholic	Episcopal	Common Lectionary
Isa. 63:16b-17 64:1-8	Isa. 63:16b-17, 19b; 64:2b-7	Isa. 64:1-9a	Isa. 63:16—64:8
1 Cor. 1:3-9	1 Cor. 1:3-9	1 Cor. 1:1-9	1 Cor. 1:3-9
Mark 13:33-37	Mark 13:33-37	Mark 13:33-37	Mark 13:32-37

ABOUT THE TEXTS

The Gospel (Mark 13:32-37) is the first text we read from Mark during this year of the second Gospel, and this pericope carries us into the heart of Markan structure and thought. It is the concluding passage of the "little apocalypse," the collection of eschatological sayings which came to be placed just before the accounts of the passion in all three Synoptic Gospels. As a collection it probably represents sayings and traditions of diverse origin in the history of the early churches. But in Mark the placement immediately before the passion account is especially significant. The community is exhorted to vigilance. But this vigilance has a specific focus: Chapters 14–16 make clear what the community is watching for.

The gospel of Mark uses conventional language for the hope of Israel. The Day or Hour of God, the time of God's salvation and God's Christ, will come. The date and manner of its arrival, however, are hidden. The community is given the parable of a watching doorkeeper as an example. Then darkness is made the very place of watching. The whole course of the night—evening, the midst of the night, cockcrow, and early morning— is to be transformed from sleep to vigilance, as if the community were doorkeeper to the house of the needy world.

But in Mark the reference to the coming day or the returning householder is not a reference outside of the book itself. *Grēgoreite,* the disciples are told in 13:35. *Grēgoreite,* the command is repeated in 13:37 to all, to the whole Christian community beyond these present disciples, to all who hear this book, to all the assemblies where the book is read: "Stay awake; pay attention," they are told. If we stay awake for just a few more verses, we find that the command is again repeated in the very next chapter (14:34, 37, 38), in the only other place this word is used in the second Gospel: *Grēgoreite,* Jesus says to the disciples in Gethsemane. Only now the

15

surprise is that the "hour" which has suddenly come, though they were not watching, is not the hour or day as conventionally expected. Peter and the others awake out of sleep to behold the cup of suffering and the arrival of the betrayer.

It seems that Mark intends this reading. All that religion hopes for in its cries for deliverance and peace does come, but under the hidden form of their contrary, in the presence of the cross. "Watch," says the apocalypse, "at evening, in the midst of the night, at cockcrow, in the early morning." If we then pay attention when we read what remains of the book, we see that it is "evening" (14:17) when Jesus gives himself at supper, interpreting and presenting the meaning of the cross, his body and the blood of the covenant, and promising the new eating in the dominion of God. It is then in the midst of the night when the "hour" comes (14:41) as an hour of betrayal. At "cockcrow" (14:72; cf. 14:30) Jesus is denied. "Early" (15:1—*prōi*) he is bound and handed over to Pilate. For Mark the passion of Jesus is the arrival of the day and salvation of God.

But we are not done watching. "Very early" on the first day of the week (16:2—*lian prōi*) the news of the resurrection is encountered. The women have become the "doorkeepers," watching now at the door of an utterly unexpected place—a tomb. It may be that the unusual way to describe the entrance to the tomb in Mark—a "door" (16:3; cf. 15:46)—is meant to alert us that the householder is coming, in the midst of death and defeat and burial. The crucified and *risen* one, who will be seen in the home places of the community where the gospel began, in the ordinary mixed world, in "Galilee" (16:7; cf. 14:28; 1:14), is himself the presence of the looked-for day of God.

Read at the outset of Advent, this text proposes that all of the December darkness, with its normal sense of waiting for the returning light, be allowed to be the night-course of the doorkeeper's watching. We receive the December festal expectation as we receive, in Mark, the ordinary language of religious eschatology. We let December's turning toward the new year become a metaphor for biblical hope.

But then, by the Markan juxtaposition, both the December waiting and the biblical hope are transformed. The light we are hoping for is present in Jesus Christ. "Watch!" now becomes, in the assembly, something like the old Byzantine deacon's cry before the reading of the Gospel: "Let us attend!" This text, when read in context in the second Gospel, pushes us forward to see the unexpected arrival of the eschaton in the account of the passion and resurrection. But, read in the assembly, it also pushes us forward to see that the very eating and drinking of the day of God is now present in the Eucharist of Christ's body and blood. Those who pay attention to the reading and the Eucharist are then trained to see and stay awake in the world. Being doorkeepers there, the community is invited to behold God's coming not simply into our December darkness, but into every darkness, at all times, and especially into places of suffering and need. The name of God's compassionate coming into the world is Jesus, the one in whom God shared unjust suffering.

The First Lesson (Isaiah 63:16b—64:8) is taken from the diverse collection which has come to be called, in scholarly writing, Third Isaiah. That is, it is one of the pieces that was joined to the Isaian corpus during the time of the restoration from exile. Specifically, this text is part of a psalm of lament and beseeching that is deeply aware of the wretched state of the returned exiles and of the destroyed temple (63:18). In the midst of such wretchedness the psalmist pleads for a theophany, for God simply to *come* as in the ancient unexpected theophanies that are told of in the tradition of the people. The psalmist pleads, in the central line: "O that you would rend the heavens and come down!" That beseeching is linked with several remarkable metaphors. Israel returned from exile is unformed clay that will be shaped by the coming of the LORD, who is the potter. The returned exiles are in such a dreadful state that neither Abraham nor Jacob, the natural fathers of Israel in the tradition, would claim them (63:16a). But the LORD will claim them as their "father," not by engendering them but simply by being with them in mercy. The faith of the psalmist is that God "meets" those who work righteousness, remembering God's ways. But now, with Israel unclean, God is hidden. There is no meeting. Thus the psalmist pleads: "Come!"

Read during Advent, this poem of Third Isaiah gives words to our waiting. "O that you would rend the heavens and come down" is a prayer that has long been used by the Christian liturgy as a central prayer and theme of Advent. The strength of this old prophetic language transforms the waiting for the sun and for the feast into a waiting for God. Even more, it links the community, through these words arising out of Israel's wretched need, to all the wretched everywhere, at every time of year, whose lives cry out for restoration and for "meeting" with God. Christian life is to be, with them and with Israel, a waiting for God.

Read next to the Gospel for today, this text deepens the tradition behind the eschatological language of Mark 13 and heightens the surprise. Here is a new "terrible thing which we looked not for": God has shared the lot of the wretched, thus rending the heavens and coming down. In Christ, those who are unclean, unformed, and fatherless, those who are outside the recognition of Abraham and Jacob, meet mercy.

The Second Lesson (1 Corinthians 1:3-9) is the opening greeting and thanksgiving of the first letter to the community at Corinth. The central theme of the thanksgiving is that "all speech and knowledge" are the form in which the grace of God in Christ sustains this community as they wait for the day of theophany, a day that is now known as "the day of our Lord Jesus Christ." The first of a series of eschatologically oriented epistle pericopes that will be read through Advent, series B, this thanksgiving also gives us speech and knowledge for interpreting the relationship of the assembly to the ancient prayer of Israel (First Lesson) and to the surprising eschatology of Mark (Gospel). We may borrow this language of an ancient community to speak about how our assembly cries out for the day of God's coming and watches for the presence of Christ. Indeed, the texts from Mark and Isaiah are made part of the testimony to Christ that is confirmed among us, part of the communion with Christ that God gives us, sustaining us and turning us toward the day. This is probably not what Paul meant, but it is not inappropriate for us to understand that, as we wait for the day, the ancient Isaian prayer and the surprising language of Mark play the same role in our community that sacred utterance and *gnōsis* did in Paul's interpretation of Corinth.

Ancient commentators on the liturgy used to speak of the "three comings" of Christ toward which Advent turns: in the incarnation, in Word and Sacrament, and at the end. Using the language of today's readings we may speak thus to our assembly: The first coming of the housekeeper through the door is in the passion and resurrection of Christ. But that coming is still hidden, having the form itself of a waiting for God: "My God, my God, why have you forsaken me," Jesus cries out (Mark 15:34). "You *will* see him," the white-robed youth promises (Mark 16:7). But watch, pay attention at the door. Now, in the community itself, there is the testimony, the speech, the supper. These speak of God's coming in the world, among the wretched poor, and so they are themselves a form of God's coming. But watch; let this second coming form you to pay attention in the world and sustain you until the hoped-for day. Live in the waiting world looking toward the promise that God's mercy is intended openly to comfort all.

The assembly, then, by the great grace of Christ, has the testimony and the language for God's coming. But it is not the only place where God will come; it is the doorkeeper, keeping watch. By such terms the church is formed in its vocation and the Christian experience of December darkness is made into a reappropriation of the deepest form of biblical hope.

AROUND THE TEXTS

"Stir up your power, O Lord, and come" we pray on this Sunday and on the Fourth Sunday in Advent. We thereby echo the urgent language of the First Lesson: "O that you would rend the heavens and come down,"

"Stir up our hearts," we pray on the Second Sunday. We thereby ask to take up the role of the watchful doorkeeper. The liturgy is full of strong symbols and words which call us into such beseeching and watching.

Some of those words are in the proper chant texts provided for the liturgy of the day (see, for example, the *Lutheran Book of Worship—Ministers Desk Edition*, pp. 121, 208). The beseeching of the First Lesson is continued and made our own with the text of Psalm 80: "Restore us, O God . . . show us the light of your face and we shall be saved" (v. 7). We turn toward the Gospel read in our midst with the same prayer, now given a christological meaning since this Verse of the day addresses the risen one in the Gospel: "Show us your steadfast love, O Lord, and give us your salvation." These are the words of people in need: ourselves, yes, but ourselves connected to the present realities of a needy world.

But the sense that the one we long for is already present is also echoed in these proper liturgical texts. As we set the table for the Eucharist, we may sing, "Salvation is at hand . . . that glory may dwell in our land." In the meal, we will taste the fruit of the land and, because of Christ's gift, at the same time we will taste the presence of the goodness and glory of God. The prayer of the meal regards the *promise* of God's coming as itself already a great comfort, a conversion of our longing into hope for all things: "You comforted your people with the promise of a Redeemer, through whom you will also make all things new. . . ."

Probably the most widely used liturgical emblem for our waiting, however, is not these words but a symbolic object: the Advent wreath. The wreath is most likely, at origin, an old pagan solstice-time symbol. A wagon wheel was hung up and decorated with greens that pointed to the hope for the returning summer by being brought indoors. These greens were used to enact the "midwinter protest." They may even have been intended to work a little "sympathetic magic": to encourage and cause vegetation again to appear. Candles or torches were affixed to the wheel. As the darkness grew so did the number of lighted torches, until at last, at the solstice itself, a full circle of such lights was aflame. Here, too, was midwinter protest and, perhaps, sympathetic magic: The circle of light was a little "sun," the burning orb, shining in midwinter.

Christians, too, have brought the burning wheel into their homes and churches. Usually they have reduced the number of candles to four, letting them stand for the Sundays of Advent. Then, if the greens and the growing circle represent the ancient human waiting for light, the burning candles themselves—even when there is only one—speak of the light of Christ already present in the midst of our waiting. The single candle of the First Sunday can be seen as strongly corresponding to the Gospel of the day: the householder comes in the darkness; the eschaton occurs in the cross.

It is better to let the wreath be such a solstice symbol, made to speak of Christ, than to tame it and trivialize it as a signboard for Christmas. The candles ought not be seen as the "prophecy candle," the "shepherd candle," the "angel candle," and the "magi candle." The wreath, rather, is one of the strongest symbols we have for the old solstice hopes. The slow completing of the circle of light has no name or text but this: the ancient human hope for the sun. Hung in the room of assembly, of preaching and sacrament, the wreath calls that hope to transformation through the word and presence of God, the burning light "which goes not down."

The Second Sunday in Advent

Lutheran	Roman Catholic	Episcopal	Common Lectionary
Isa. 40:1-11	Isa. 40:1-5, 9-11	Isa. 40:1-11	Isa. 40:1-11
2 Pet. 3:8-14	2 Pet. 3:8-14	2 Pet. 3:8-15a, 18	2 Pet. 3:8-15a
Mark 1:1-8	Mark 1:1-8	Mark 1:1-8	Mark 1:1-8

ABOUT THE TEXTS

The Gospel (Mark 1:1-8) for this Sunday is the initial paragraph of the Gospel of Mark. This first paragraph is read in Advent in order to begin our full reading of the second Gospel during the coming church year, in order to begin at the beginning. It is also read in order to set John the Baptist before us as a key figure in the interpretation of Advent.

This first paragraph opens with words that sound like a title. Indeed, like the title and opening sentences of any carefully written work, this phrase reveals much about the work itself, even offering to the attentive reader a disclosure of the book's core meaning. In the other Gospels such a title does not occur. But in Mark, the word gospel, used in primitive Christianity for the *oral* proclamation of the good news of Christ, is actually used in the text as the title for the book. Or, to put the matter more accurately, the word is used as *part* of the title of the book, "the beginning (*archē*) of the gospel" (i.e., "the beginning of the proclaimed good news").

One might understand this title as referring simply to what follows in the rest of this pericope. There is much to commend such an understanding. The texts about a promised precursor and the ministry of the Baptist are then understood to be part of the gospel itself, its very beginning. The prophets and the Baptist begin the preaching. Promise, preparation, hoping, and waiting are themselves understood to be part of the proclamation of eschatological arrival.

But when one sees that there is no clear break after this first pericope, no "chapter one" that is the gospel itself after this "introduction" to the gospel, the suspicion grows that the title is the title of the whole book. Indeed, we have already noted (see "About the Texts" for the First Sunday in Advent) that the climax of the book, and not just the first paragraph, has the form of waiting. If, in Mark, the cross is the arrival of the day of God, it is also publicly a cry to heaven. If, in Mark, the resurrection is the eschatological event, it also is not yet seen. "You *will* see him," the youth promises the women in the next to last verse of chapter 16. Here too, then, waiting and hiddenness are understood to be part of arrival. The first paragraph prefigures the core of the whole book. The book is the beginning of the gospel. The gospel itself is the encounter with the risen one, "seeing" him, in the present assembly, the present proclamation.

Of course, *archē* means more than "beginning." It is also "ground" and "principle," even our "core meaning." Say it this way then: "The basic principle of the gospel of Jesus Christ." Let that be the title of the book. Such a title would mean that when the text is read today, the one who is hidden in the events the text recounts is revealed to us. We know the identity of the one who was unrecognized in the ambiguous preaching of John, in the stories of the hidden messiah, in the cross, and even in the Markan account of the resurrection. In the very first sentence we are told he is "the son of God." That sentence becomes the principle of the rest of the book. We hear it and are thereby given the key to understanding even when the disciples misunderstand. The text, full of accounts of preparation and suffering and yet full of the revelation to us of Jesus' true identity, is the ground of the gospel.

It is not only Jesus who is hidden and revealed in the book. John the Baptist's identity also seems to be hidden in the events and revealed to us. John appears in the text as the tradition has known him, a figure of late Jewish apocalypticism. His deeds fit easily with what we know from other sources about the many figures who longingly proclaimed the hope of God's coming in a situation of cruelty and military oppression. His baptism is not just a sign of regret, a change of mind about God and sin, a personal religious act. It is a full-hearted communal turning, in an aching and unclean time, toward the hope for God's coming. It is standing in the old water of deliverance, the Jordan, the water the people crossed in order to claim the land as God's. It is crying out to God for that same deliverance anew. The spirit baptism John promises is to be the coming of the day itself, when the Spirit is poured out, for good or ill, on all flesh. But in fact, it was not the Spirit but the Roman and Herodian soldiers that continued to descend upon John and upon those hoping people. This figure of John speaks with a moving, but dead voice from the past, bearing witness to old agonies, bringing us to see a consolation that never came.

But, if we pay attention, we hear something else besides. In Mark's Gospel, ancient texts from Isaiah (40:3) and Malachi (3:1) are linked to John. It is not so much that he is the "fulfillment" of these prophetic texts (which Mark calls collectively "Isaiah"), as that he is presented to us today as the lively presence of these old words. In fact, to us hearers he takes on the words. Because of the second text (Isaiah 40), the promise of a voice in the wilderness announcing the return of God, Mark says to us that John appears in the *wilderness*. This is an odd place for baptizing (we thought he was at the Jordan!), but it is the very place that the prophet promises will be full of water (cf. Isaiah 35) and of the coming of the Lord. And because of the Isaiah text, Mark says that John preaches baptism (an odd verb to link with baptism!) as if baptism were the word of preparation for the Lord's coming. Because of the first text (Mal. 3:1), the promise of a messenger, of Elijah come back again before the great day of God (cf. Mal. 4:5), Mark tells us that John is clothed with Elijah's characteristic garb (2 Kings 1:8) and eats the kosher food of the wild (Lev. 11:22; 1 Sam. 14:25).

We hear of a pathetic apocalyptic figure from the past. We listen again. It is Elijah and the blossoming wilderness. This should not surprise us, for the baptism that people underwent, hoping for and turning toward the day of God, is not dead. It is still done in our midst. It still turns toward God's day, only now in the name of Jesus and in the power of the outpoured Spirit.

John is hidden as a figure of the hope of the oppressed. He is hidden, described in the terms of conventional religious expectation. Finally, he is hidden in death. The one who promised God's coming is done away with, imprisoned, beheaded. He becomes another figure of failed religious hope, his baptism the sign of an old cry for God. But Mark's Gospel claims that it is *Elijah* they killed (Mark 9:13), the precursor of the Day of God. That is revealed to us in the Markan text as surely as it is revealed that Jesus is the Coming One, prefigured by John and also killed. In Mark the old apocalyptic figure becomes part of the beginning of the gospel now proclaimed to us. The waters of baptism, which still flow here, are made the way of God's coming.

Thus it is not just the identity of Jesus or of John or the meaning of baptism that is revealed in the assembly; it is God. If John baptized, expressing the need of the people, and if Jesus was crucified, crying out that need, we are told that these needy signs at the Jordan were the acts of Elijah and this crucifixion is the very coming of God. For the "beginning of the gospel" pairs the events of the book with the promise and presence of the Holy One of Israel. According to the texts that are summoned, Elijah is to precede *God* and the voice in the wilderness is to cry out before the returning LORD. We may assume that the mighty one who will pour out the Spirit as a final baptism is also none other than God. But we know that it is *Jesus* who comes after John and that *his* final baptism is suffering and death (10:38). By the occurrence of the gospel in the assembly, by the proclamation and presence that begins with this Gospel book, we are invited to trust that this coming of Jesus among our need is the coming of God.

When this text is read in Advent, a transformation can occur in our experience of the December darkness and in our experience of time itself. Waiting is seen as an appropriate stance for the people of God in every time, not only in December. The baptisms we enact are themselves a form of waiting, a crying out for God. The sufferings of the people who went out to John in the text may become a bridge for us to know ourselves linked to all the wretched of the earth whose lives cry out and wait for God. But the gospel in our midst now announces that the one who shared our lot is already the coming of God's day, of God's return. Baptism in his name is now both the truth of human suffering and entry into the presence of the dominion of God. On, in, and under our waiting we find already the one we hoped for, waiting for us! Encouraged by this text, we make the reading of Mark, of "the beginning of the gospel," the occasion for the gospel itself in preaching and in the Supper.

Advent is like John the Baptist. It is an old, even odd custom. It speaks a customary language of religious expectation, turning toward the light. Its power among us comes from the fact that people are suffering, hoping for something better. But paired with the biblical texts, as John goes paired with texts from the prophets in our pericope, Advent turns not simply toward the solstice feast but toward the presence of eternal mercy in our midst. Paired with the gospel of Jesus Christ, Advent itself becomes a precursor and preacher of the gospel. Indeed, filled with the presence of Christ in the midst of the assembly, Advent becomes part of the gospel.

The First Lesson (Isaiah 40:1-11) is the full text from Second Isaiah from which is drawn one of the quotations at the beginning of Mark. In its original context it is a magnificent announcement of the end of the exile. In fact, it is probably to be understood as the prologue and beginning of the collection of Second Isaiah, the themes of which are announced here: the comfort of the return from exile and the sureness of the word of God. The text may even represent the call of the prophet to speak that word. In that case, the voices of the text include the reluctant "I" of the prophet (40:6) but also unnamed voices (40:3, 6) from the heavenly council or from among the angelic messengers of God. The prophet is ordained to speak promise to the abandoned city, to announce that a way will be made through the wilderness, and to herald the return of God, following and carrying the exiles. This "speaking" is heard from heaven. It is not mortal, dying speech, but a sure and enduring word. To hear it is already to begin to experience God's return.

Read in Advent, this text offers the old hope of the return from exile as another biblical image to deepen the connections of December waiting. Even more, it calls us to rely upon the sureness of the many texts of promise we will hear in these days. The whole of Advent is to be sung out as a kind of comfort to all the people.

Read next to the Gospel for today, this pericope strengthens the astonishing revelation of Mark. John, the baptizer amidst the need of the people, is not just any voice come before the coming of God. His baptizing is heard as a voice from the heavenly council itself, promising the merciful coming of God and commissioning us all as heralds. The Second Sunday in Advent finds its biblical center in the beginning and principal word of Second Isaiah set next to the beginning and core meaning of the Gospel of Mark. Both texts heighten expectation and begin to fulfill their own promise.

The Second Lesson (2 Peter 3:8-14) can symbolize the church gathering around this biblical center. Today, Mark and Second Isaiah give us the primary words for the coming of God. This passage from a late pseudepigraphic Christian writing attributed to Peter urges us to "wait for and earnestly desire" that coming, to turn toward it with our lives, and not to lose heart at the delay, remembering God's own sense of time. The text also gathers the very earth and heavens themselves into our hoping. "We wait for a new heavens and a new earth in which righteousness dwells." The comforting word of the heavenly council spoken to Jerusalem through the prophet is now extended to all things. Although this newness comes through fire, it is nonetheless a newness promised to earth and heaven.

We need to read that promise with care. Ancient solstice festivities have always celebrated hope for the earth and for its fertility. Advent and Christmas should be no different. We desperately need such celebration today. But the pagan celebrations may have seemed to suggest that the coming of summer was enough renewal, the gods of the fertile earth enough of the divine. In a time of nuclear threat, the "greenhouse effect," and acid rain, we are aware that cries for the earth are cries for a larger mercy than that which will come automatically in the turning seasons. And those who cry for the earth must turn toward that mercy in lives of care and respect for the earth.

On the other hand, Christians have sometimes read of the promised fire as if its coming means that there need be no concern for the earth. Indeed, some have even asserted that our bombs may be used as the final destroying fire. Such assertions are blasphemy. That the new earth comes through fire is a biblical metaphor for its coming only through the unexpected action of God, through the power of God's creating Spirit. The newness we hope for and are invited to live toward comes from God, not from the simple turning of the seasons nor from our rejection of the earth.

AROUND THE TEXTS

The voice of John the Baptist is heard throughout the liturgy of Advent. If we turn toward Christ present in the Gospel today, singing the proper Verse, we hear John speaking as if he were the heavenly voice of Isaiah 40: "Prepare the way of the Lord." If we sing Psalm 85 as a way to receive the First Lesson, John's function and preaching is recalled: "Righteousness shall go before him, and peace shall be a pathway for his feet." Hymns today will most likely take John as a central figure: "On Jordan's bank the Baptist's cry announces that the Lord is nigh." And throughout December one may find other figures of the church's commemoration—Nicholas, Ambrose, Lucy, John of the Cross and Teresa of Avila, Thomas the Apostle—speaking like the Baptist, preparing the way and inviting us to see already the light that transforms our darkness.

But a more powerful way to let our liturgy fulfill the function of the Baptist is to keep it spare. The simplicity—even austerity—and the waiting silence of the Advent liturgy may be an immensely important symbol of our connection to a waiting world. The liturgy may be like John's "wilderness," the spare and empty place that will blossom and fill with water at God's return. The silences after preaching and before praying might be lengthened now. The *Kyrie* might be fully sung, enunciating the hopes throughout the world to which this community is connected. The *Gloria in Excelsis* or other hymn of praise might be suppressed. The minor keys and solo instruments might be heard in the congregation's music. It will be as if the silence between the words and sounds is as important as the words and sounds themselves.

Such a silence and spareness in church is an important gift the assembly can give to a world anxious to celebrate too quickly. The waiting of the liturgy speaks a truth about the world—and about each person—that people deeply long to hear. The salvation of God that comes to our darkest places cannot be sufficiently expressed if we only use lavish celebration and major keys as the modes of proclamation. Christmas decorations and Christmas music and Christmas pageants are not to be excluded from too-early use in the church because we are pretending to be people before the incarnation, but because *we* need Advent. Spareness and silence are honest to us. And, if we are learning from the Gospel of Mark, spareness and silence can be most eloquent modes for the proclamation of the gospel of Jesus Christ *today*.

The Third Sunday in Advent

Lutheran	Roman Catholic	Episcopal	Common Lectionary
Isa. 61:1-3, 10-11	Isa. 61:1-2a, 10-11	Isa. 65:17-25	Isa. 61:1-4, 8-11
1 Thess. 5:16-24	1 Thess. 5:16-24	1 Thess. 5:16-28	1 Thess. 5:16-24
John 1:6-8, 19-28	John 1:6-8, 19-28	John 1:6-8, 19-28	John 1:6-8, 19-28

ABOUT THE TEXTS

The Gospel (John 1:6-8, 19-28) for this Sunday again proposes John the Baptist as a key figure in the Christian interpretation and transformation of December waiting. While making use of themes we have already encountered in the Markan presentation of the Baptist, this pericope adds significant Johannine themes and allows the precursor's witness to be heard in a new way. The intention of the evangelist was to introduce his book, turning the Baptist's work into a testimony to the one the Gospel was about to proclaim. The result for us, when this text is read on this Sunday, is that the Baptist's witness transforms our Advent.

We have already observed in Mark (see the commentary on the Gospel for the Second Sunday in Advent) how the Baptist was made part of the beginning and ground of the gospel itself. The same work is accomplished in the Fourth Gospel, not simply by placing John at the outset (v. 19), immediately after the prologue, but also by interweaving sentences about John (vv. 6-8, 15) into the material from the hymn that the Fourth Evangelist remolded into a poetic introduction to and summary of the whole work. In fact, the name of the Baptist is the only name we encounter in the prologue until the contrasting names of Moses and Jesus Christ are set out in a great climax to the poem (v. 17). While Mark's *"archē* of the gospel" (Mark 1:1) includes John the Baptist, the *archē* of the Fourth Gospel articulates the very beginning of all things, echoing the first verses of Genesis in astonishing christological praise, but also still including the witness of John the Baptist. Given this heightening of the *archē*, the meaning of John the Baptist is also heightened. He is not simply a baptizer dealing with people's needs who is depicted as Elijah. He is now a witness to the light, to the life and *logos* at the center of the cosmos.

We have also seen in Mark that the Baptist can be called the "voice," the unnamed speaker, probably a divine voice from the heavenly council, who speaks the word of God in the initiatory vocation of Second Isaiah (Isa. 40:3). The same designation is used here, in the first pericope (1:19-28) to follow the prologue. Only now the Markan identification, made by means of pairing the figure of John preaching in the wilderness with the quotation from Isaiah, is asserted directly (1:23). That direct assertion is made into a refusal of any title of religious expectation. The unnamed character of the voice in Isaiah gives the evangelist the grounds to deny easy identification of John in any religious system. Just as in the prologue John is not the light, so also in this first pericope John confesses that he is not the Christ, Elijah, or the prophet. John is simply the voice, which is to say, he is the lively presence of the scriptural promise. He is the presence of the still valid word spoken in the heavenly council. He is not the next robed figure to appear in a divine drama of holy history. There is no interest here in details of John's biography or his personality or even his historical significance. What matters is the voice, and the voice denies.

That denial is at the core of our text. While John's answers are manifestly a denial, the text asserts that they are not. The refusal of titles is a *confession* (*hōmologēsen*, 1:20), that is, a public acknowledgment, often of religious or judicial importance. The repeated insistence on John's speech as *homologia* only strengthens the denial. To encounter John is already to encounter the destruction of religious categories. That Elijah must come first or that John must be somebody important in sacred history—these beliefs do not hold here, before the actual coming of God. The confession of the Baptist in 1:19-23 plays out the denial of the prologue: "He was not the light."

"But he came to bear witness to the light." The denial-confession of John prepares us to see how John's witness also plays out a further theme of the prologue. The initial poem says of the Word, "The world knew him not." In our pericope John, speaking about his own baptizing, bears witness to the presence of the unknown light. At this point in the Markan text John speaks of the eschatological Spirit to be poured on all the earth. John's baptism is seen to go before and prefigure that outpouring. We, the hearers of the Markan Gospel, come to know that the coming one who will pour out the Spirit is none other than the crucified, and that John's baptism, indeed, prefigures the cross. The Fourth Gospel makes a similar point in a very different way. "I have baptized you with water, but the one who is coming will baptize you with the Holy Spirit" (Mark 1:8) is replaced with "I baptize with water; but among you stands one whom you do not know" (John 1:26). The eschatological presence of the coming one is confessed, and that coming one stands in the midst of baptism. But his meaning transcends our placing him within accepted categories and taming him. If John, the witness to the light, breaks out of all religious meanings, how much more does the light itself? To encounter Christ is to receive grace upon grace and to come to know God. It is not to comprehend and control Christ, who is life and light for us in the unexpected place that is the cross.

Our text, then, is made up of some of the verses about the Baptist that the Fourth Gospel has interwoven in the prologue (1:6-8) together with the first pericope that follows the prologue (1:19-28). The themes from the prologue are unfolded in the first pericope; thus John is "not the light" (1:8) and the testimony of John is the denial-confession (1:20-21). But John is a witness to the light (1:7-8) and John is the voice bearing witness to the presence of the unknown one amidst John's baptizing (1:23, 26-27). The uncategorizable John is seen to prefigure the unknowable Jesus. But as the John who is not Elijah or the Christ is heard by us as the very voice of heaven, so the unknown and unreceived Jesus is met in this assembly, and the meeting is endless grace.

Read in Advent, this text invites us to let the December waiting for the sun and the feast of the sun become a waiting for God. We are asked to look beyond the sun we hope for, but also beyond all the titles and observances of religion. What our December and our religion long for we cannot name or give ourselves. It is God and God's grace. Let our darkness wait for *that* light. John is present in our Advent as Advent itself says, "I am not Elijah or the prophet." Let the darkness of December refuse all titles but the very coming of God. John is present in our Advent not as we talk about him but as the voice of witness is present. Let December say: "Make straight the way of the Lord."

It is interesting that the calculation theory of the origin of Christmas places the feast at the winter solstice in relationship to biblical accounts of the birth of the Baptist. The festival of the nativity of John the Baptist is on June 24, the old date for the summer solstice, which is the time of the greatest light in the northern hemisphere. But as the world's light wanes towards the time of greatest darkness at the winter solstice, we come to the feast of the true Light, brighter than the sun, given in the midst of our darkness. We come to the feast of the incarnation, of the encounter with grace upon grace in the light of God. The Johannine John the Baptist says, "He must increase, but I must decrease" (3:28). Advent is like John when its continuing decrease of light is made to bear witness to the coming of God's grace in the midst of our need. John is present in our Advent when we know this about our observances and our days: They are not the light.

But it is not that we simply turn toward the still coming God. The transcendent one, the unknown and unreceived one, is in our midst, now. By God's mercy Jesus Christ *is* received and we encounter grace. We do not simply wait for Christmas, or for something beyond Christmas. Advent is not playacting, pretending to be the people waiting for the Messiah. The waiting that Christians do, connected to the waiting poor of the world who wait still for the full and open manifestation of God's mercy, ought not be trivialized in such a way. We let the December darkness be a strong and evocative symbol of our larger waiting, but we do not pretend to be living in a time other than we actually now are. Every Sunday assembly, even and especially during Advent, is a gathering in the power of the Spirit and in the presence of the risen Christ before the revealed face of God. "Waiting" is our human condition. Encounter and revelation and grace are God's gift. This text heightens our waiting, turning us toward God and connecting us to the darkness that at every time of year and in all religious systems waits for the transcendent one. But this text is read at Sunday Eucharist, where the risen one holds out his wounds and invites us to recognize him.

The First Lesson (Isaiah 61:1-3, 10-11) takes us again to the final poems of the Isaian collection, the songs, prayers, and exhortations at the time of the return from exile that are sometimes called Third Isaiah. Isaiah 61 is such a song, written in the manner of the Servant Songs of Second Isaiah, but celebrating the great joy of the return.

In verses 1-3 of our text, the prophet speaks, exulting in his vocation. The afflicted, brokenhearted captives to whom he is to speak are the exiles returned and returning. In fact, this text may again represent an inaugural prophetic vision, "the call" of a new prophet in the Isaian tradition. The task of the prophet is to announce a real jubilee year, real comfort from God, in the return of the exiles to a rebuilding city and a renewed vocation for Israel.

The response in verses 10-11 is probably best understood as the speech of the city itself and all its inhabitants. The city understands itself as clothed in God's regard, in salvation, as bridegroom and bride are clothed for a wedding. While elsewhere the city may be understood as the bride of God, here the city is simply clothed in great festivity as if it were going to the nuptials of God with the earth. Indeed, the earth itself celebrates, for the very growing of grass and garden are metaphors for the appearance of God's mercy in the sight of all the nations.

We are used to this text in Christian circles, since it is so closely linked to the beginning of Jesus' ministry according to the Gospel of Luke. Indeed, in the Lutheran lectionary, verses from Isaiah 61 are read together with the beginning of the sermon at Nazareth (Luke 4) on the Third Sunday after Epiphany in Year C. Here, in the midst of Advent, however, the intention of the text is slightly different. This Sunday is the old *Gaudete* Sunday, a day of rejoicing halfway through Advent. The text means to celebrate that joy. In the face of the "exiles" in the congregation, let the preacher of the day have the vocation of the prophet. Let comfort, garlands, gladness, anointing, clothing be spoken. In the face of the need in the world, let the church have the vocation to speak such rich comfort. Then let the assembly sing for the world the response of the city, our baptismal robe already being the garment with which God intends to clothe the world, our Eucharist already being the wedding feast of God with all things. The joy of Advent, the joy of an anticipation in the midst of which God already dwells, sings out in this text. The old solstitial hope for the fruitful earth is given a biblical interpretation as, in this text, the earth itself rejoices in God's salvation.

Read next to the Gospel of the day, the First Lesson helps us to see that the vocation of John the Baptist, and therefore the vocation of Advent itself and of Advent preachers, is the vocation of the prophet in Third Isaiah. The presence of the light in the midst of the world, the presence of the unknown one, gives us the grounds for claiming the joy of the Isaiah text. Jesus Christ, in the midst of the darkness and waiting of the world, crucified and risen, is the garland on the earth's brow, the springing forth of the garden's shoots. His cross and his coming again in our midst are the ground of hope for the earth.

Because of the close relationship of this text to the Luke 4 passage, the Episcopal lectionary chooses another joyful passage from Third Isaiah as the First Lesson *(Isaiah 65:17-25)*. Here God speaks, but the themes are very similar to those in Isaiah 61. The city comes into festal joy and peace. The futility of early death and warfare is banished. Long life is promised. Such a text might be regarded as an elaboration of the prophet's vocation in Isaiah 61 and used similarly to unfold the message of the Baptist and of Advent. What comes to even stronger expression in Isaiah 65, however, making it a fine alternative reading, is the participation of the world itself in the salvation of God. Both cosmological macrocosm—"a new heavens and a new earth"—and zoological microcosm—the wolf and the lamb, lion and ox—show forth the life-giving intention of God.

The Second Lesson (1 Thessalonians 5:16-24) is the concluding verses of the First Letter to the Thessalonians. The key words, which pulled the reading to this Sunday, are clearly the first ones: "Rejoice always." But here is also the promise that the whole human being, described in comprehensive words of wholeness, is to be kept unaccused at the "coming" of Jesus Christ. And here in the text is the strong liturgical presence of the local community: The text is meant for the assembly, as if it were the actual presence of the apostle. It comes with words of prayer and greetings of peace and grace. It is to be accompanied with the holy kiss.

As this text is read in the assembly today we let it evoke our local community, our reading of the apostolic texts, our prayers, our kiss of peace, our *eucharistia*. Because of the voice of John, the message of the prophet, made living to us in the presence of the risen Christ, we too are invited to trust that God's promise is for the whole human being. We too are invited to see that the will of God for the assembly in the midst of the current darkness is that it rejoice, pray, give thanks, and so bear witness to God in the world. The rejoicing assembly of the Thessalonian letter has a mood very much like the city in Third Isaiah. The city, the Thessalonian congregation, and the present liturgical assembly all have the same task: to bear witness in joy to the intention of God with the earth.

AROUND THE TEXTS

Sometime in the week following this Sunday we will come to the day of the beginning of the old Roman Saturnalia, December 17. By one theory (see Introduction above) Advent originated as a Christian counterobservance to this festival and other festivals of the year's turning. It may be that this old opposition is recalled by the fact that on December 17 the medieval Western church began to sing a special series of texts, celebrating the rich mercy of God in Christ and beseeching that mercy to come.

These texts are called the "O Antiphons" (for a current version, see, for example, the *Lutheran Book of Worship—Ministers Desk Edition*, pp. 92–93). Their most widespread version is probably the hymnic paraphrase, "O Come, O Come Emmanuel." Originally, however, they were single antiphons sung at Evening Prayer, on each of these last days of Advent, before and after the communal singing of Mary's Song, Luke 1:46-55. Mary's Song was thus emphasized, making its eschatological language about God's present action available to interpret our Advent prayer. And Vespers was intensified in its beseeching for the present intervention of God's mercy.

It is remarkable to note that the "psalm" for today, sung in response to the First Lesson and its joy, is none other than Mary's Song. It is even more important to note that this very Sunday, in which the Baptist refuses all names and Jesus is called "one whom you do not know," introduces the week in which these antiphons might be used, perhaps now simply as a responsive prayer. For the series of seven antiphons is none other than a rich chain of biblical names addressed to Jesus: Wisdom, Adonai, Root of Jesse, Key of David, Dayspring (the rising sun), King of nations, and Emmanuel. All of these texts beseech Christ to come. The one whom we do not know is progressively encountered in these texts, until at last we meet him as "God with us."

The Fourth Sunday in Advent

Lutheran	Roman Catholic	Episcopal	Common Lectionary
2 Sam. 7:1-11, 16	2 Sam. 7:1-5, 8b-12, 14a, 16	2 Sam. 7:4, 8-16	2 Sam. 7:8-16
Rom. 16:25-27	Rom. 16:25-27	Rom. 16:25-27	Rom. 16:25-27
Luke 1:26-38	Luke 1:26-38	Luke 1:26-38	Luke 1:26-38

ABOUT THE TEXTS

The Gospel (Luke 1:26-38) for this day brings the account of the annunciation to Mary into the celebration of Advent. While it may seem odd to follow two Sundays in which John the Baptist functions as a central figure with the account of an event that occurs before John's birth, that is only true if one regards Advent as a progressive drama of past holy history. If one regards the Sundays of the season, rather, as the proclamation of Christ into the present need, symbolized by the darkness of the year, then Mary rightly follows John. John bears witness. Mary receives and assents to the presence of the Word.

Furthermore, when the annunciation text follows the witness of John the Baptist, the purpose of the text itself becomes clearer. At its core, the account is not about the pregnant Mary, her history, or her virginity. It is not an occasion to give Mary a week-long pregnancy in a drama that leads to Christmas. It is a christological text. It gives deeper significance to the one to whom John pointed. The text means to proclaim to us, in the words of the strong angel of God, who Christ is. It means to set that proclamation over against the festivities of the world, calling people to find in this heir of David a stronger renewal of hope for the world than the solstice can ever give. And to that witness the text invites us to respond as the believing Mary: "Let it be to me according to your word."

It is fascinating to find that the text itself "follows" John the Baptist. The dating of the pericope is in relationship to John: The "sixth month" of the text (1:26, 36) is the sixth month of Elizabeth's pregnancy, the sixth month since the angel announced John's birth. The pattern of the annunciation itself (angel's presence, fear, "do not be afraid," description of the promised child in scriptural terms, question, sign given) follows the pattern of the annunciation of John's birth (1:8-23). In Luke, in yet a different way than Mark or John, the forerunner also is made to prefigure Jesus. The Baptist is made part of the beginning of the gospel. In Mark, the Baptist is killed and then Jesus is killed, and we are told that in doing this the world has in fact slain Elijah and the Messiah. In John, the Baptist is "not the light" and has no name, and Jesus is "one whom you do not know." In Luke, the Baptist is announced by an angel, that is, he is seen as having his origin wholly in the mercy and gift of God. So is Jesus.

There are differences between the two annuciation accounts, of course. With John, a barren couple conceives (like ancient Hannah and Elkanah, the parents of Samuel), and the annunciation is to the man who is a priest. With Jesus, the gracious and free character of the gift of God is heightened: The annunciation is to the woman who is a virgin. In the annunciation to Zechariah there is no greeting. To Mary there is the remarkable greeting, "Hail, O favored one, the Lord is with you," which strengthens the sense of God's election and action. Zechariah's question is treated as unbelief and his silence is the resulting sign. Mary's question, however, which is of the very same kind, is graciously answered. The witnessing sign is the conception of John, and Mary is not silenced. Although she too is a questioner, by the presence of the promise she is enabled to answer with faith (cf. 1:45).

The differences in the texts correspond to the idea that John is the forerunner while Jesus is the event and presence of the mercy of God. Jesus unlocks speech and transforms doubts and questions. The response to Jesus is to be faith. That Zechariah is silent and waiting, that Elizabeth hides herself and waits (1:24), says something about the meaning of John the Baptist: As in all four Gospels, he is seen as the witness, wholly turned toward Jesus. That Mary *speaks* says something about her child: By the power of the Spirit, he is the ground of faith.

Our text, then, is about the meaning of the presence of Jesus in the world. The center of the pericope is found in the scripturally colored speech of the angel, describing the meaning of the promised one. The other material of the text—the greeting, the virginity of the mother, the action of the

Spirit, the faith of Mary—all serve to underscore the divine importance of this announced meaning of Jesus.

That meaning can be said rather simply: Jesus is the Davidic Messiah. Unlike the Gospels of Mark and John, the third Gospel is not given to the love of paradox. The speech here, as elsewhere in Luke, is direct, if poetic. "Of the house of David," a phrase used to describe Joseph (1:27) at the outset of the text, prepares us to hear Gabriel recall the promises to David's house in his description of Jesus. We hear the echo of these texts from the oracle of Nathan the prophet: "I will make for you a great name" (2 Sam. 7:9); "I will be his father, and he shall be my son" (2 Sam. 7:14); "I will establish the throne of your offspring's dominion forever" (2 Sam. 7:13); "And your house and your dominion shall be made sure for ever before me; your throne shall be established forever" (2 Sam. 7:16). And we hear the echo of a later oracle, probably spoken at the investiture (not the birth) of some ancient Judean king and included in Isaiah: "To us a child is born, to us a son is given. . . . Of the increase of his government and of peace there will be no end, upon the throne and dominion of David, to establish it . . . from this time forth and for evermore" (Isa. 9:6-7). The point is clear. In Jesus the promise of the peaceful and everlasting dominion, the just and holy monarch, will at last be realized.

There is no paradox here. The text does not note what immediately occurs to us—that nothing is said of *Mary* being "of David's house" and that Joseph is not the father! It does not matter. The promise is the word and work of God, not the accomplishment of human generation. "Of his father David" is a scriptural convention for the king. So is the title "son of God" or "son of the Most High." Like many ancient Near Eastern monarchs, the king in Israel and Judah was regarded as invested with divine sonship (cf. Ps. 2:7; Ps. 89:26-27). Jesus is to be that king. But, as in the other Synoptics, Luke finds in this old title for the anointed messiah-king a hidden witness to the actual identity of Jesus, and this witness is strengthened by the account of a virginal conception: God is his "progenitor"; he comes from God.

Luke is not above including, later in his account, a relatively unchanged form of the paradoxical Markan pericope questioning the Davidic origin of the messiah (Luke 20:41-44; Mark 12:35-37). Even our text is not finally about the Davidic *origin* of Jesus. It is about Jesus being from God. It is about the sureness of the word of God, spoken here by Gabriel, "the mighty warrior of God," the one who stands in God's very presence (1:19), the interpreter of the sure intentions of God with the world (Dan. 8:16; 9:21). It is about the ancient word being realized in the presence of Jesus in the world. Mary's faith is a response to that word "spoken to her from the Lord" (1:45), from the very presence of God.

If the texts for the preceding two Sundays invite our assembly and our observance of Advent to be formed in the pattern of the witness of John the Baptist, this Sunday's Gospel makes us to be as Mary, greeted with the presence of God, given the word of God, and responding with faith. In Nazareth, in Mary's presence, stands the angel, speaking. The angel's word does what it says: The child is conceived; the unending dominion of peace begins to be present. In our assembly the Gospel is read and preached. The Supper is celebrated. These are the sure word from the presence of God. In them we encounter the presence of Jesus Christ whose throne is the cross and whose dominion is meant for all the world. These are the angelic word for us. Then, at repeated junctures in the liturgy—when we gather at the outset, when we come to make the thanksgiving of the table— we are greeted like Mary: *Ho kurios meta sou,* says the angel. *Dominus vobiscum,* "the Lord be with you," "the Lord is with you," says the liturgy. The word which follows such exchange tells us of God's great grace and favor to the lowly, invites us to let fear go, and assures us of the core biblical mystery—that the God who raises the dead and creates something out of nothing is able to give life where there is none. That word of creative favor and life is the presence of Jesus Christ in Word and Sacrament. We are invited to respond: "Let it be to me according to your word."

This text, then, gives us the deep meaning of what occurs in every Sunday liturgy, throughout the year, even when the themes of the annunciation are not present in the readings. But today, when these themes are explicit, it is important that they not be dissipated as if this Sunday were only "getting ready for Christmas." When the annunciation of the angel is read in Advent, it speaks with authority today. It proclaims the presence of God's mercy in the midst of our current darkness and waiting. It announces the presence of Christ to us. It invites us to faith. On the final Sunday of Advent, with the darkness still great around us, we are enabled to let go of the silence of Zechariah and the hiddenness of Elizabeth and openly assent to the Word in faith. Advent has its own function in juxtaposing waiting and the Word to the world's festival of lights in the darkness. Such juxtaposition is then the best sort of getting ready for Christmas.

The First Lesson (2 Samuel 7:1-11, 16) is the principal text from which the Davidic imagery of Gabriel's speech has been drawn. This oracle of Nathan may well be part of the earliest material from which the books of Samuel have been composed. It seems to have functioned originally as part of the royal ideology, certifying and underscoring the prerogatives of the Davidic kings. With the failure of the kings, it is no wonder that it should come to provide language for the hope for a future messiah who would fulfill the expectations that kings awaken but never answer.

The actual exchange of the text involves a wordplay on "house" and an active commerce of blessing and reward between God and David. David, dwelling in a house of cedar, wants to build God a "house," that is, a fixed temple. Nathan assents, saying, "the LORD is with you" (7:3). God, on the other hand, says no. Rather, "the LORD will make you a house," that is, a lasting dynasty (7:11; cf. 7:27). David's child, however, who will be king after David and who will therefore be called God's son, will be enabled to build the temple, "a house for my name" (7:13). David responds with assent and praise and with the petition that this word be confirmed forever.

We ought to read this material of royal ideology with great care. Both kingship and the temple that came with kingship are matters of ambiguous value in the Scriptures. Solomon did indeed build a house for God—and this text may have been conceived partly as rationale both for Solomon's building and for his absolute rule. Solomon was an oriental king, and oriental kingship was strongly linked with the patron god's temple. But the house Solomon built, like all his building projects, was created with massive forced labor. Both this forced labor and the subsequent role of the temple in the religio-political centralization of the kingdom played roles in the disunity and decay of the nation. We should read this text to know something of the powerful ancient hopes for order, identity, and peace that focused upon kings. We should also hear the weeping and failure behind and following the text.

Both kingship and temple provide centrally important metaphors for the message of the New Testament. The present Sunday's Gospel is evidence of that. Even stronger and more widespread evidence is found in the christological titles, "Christ" and "Son of God," perhaps even in the tradition of calling God "Father." But here, too, care must be exercised. The tradition of royal ideology is only received in the New Testament with critique and massive transformation. We cannot continue to use the language of royal oracles without that transformation. For us, it is the crucified who is "king," the center of order and peace and God's presence. Moreover he is "king" without being any king at all, but by being the *victim* of kings. It is a virgin girl, not a mighty warrior or a royal prophet, who receives the new royal oracle. And the house of God is her temple, the body of her child, and the house of the church. This house is there for all people, welcoming the least ones into the center, into the presence of God.

Read next to the Gospel of the day and read in Advent, this text is brought to that transformation. The old royal hopes have their power. Let them stand for the hopes of people everywhere for order and peace. Let them be connected to the hopes of our people in the darkness of Advent. But let the failure and disappointment of kings also be remembered, the murderous use of their absolute control in the name of whatever god. Let us thereby know that our religious hope for "a savior king" is also not only infantile but potentially dangerous. Then let us hear the transforming word of God. In our midst is a "king" unlike all kings, bringing the eternal "reign" of God. And the Spirit is building the house for the encounter with God, first in Mary, and then in this assembly where the word is read, preached, and eaten.

The psalm which may be sung as a response to the First Lesson (Ps. 89:1-4, 14-18) prepares for this transformation of language. The psalm itself is part of the royal ideology, a celebration of the very material we find in Nathan's oracle. In liturgical use, however, the psalm is edited so that the royal language, while still present, is subtly turned to celebrate the steadfast and loving promise of God rather than the prerogatives of the king. The liturgy intends to turn the old royal hopes toward a new kind of "throne" and a new kind of "rule." When we sing, "Righteousness and justice are the foundations of your throne; love and truth go before your face," we begin to hear the royal ideology set next to the Gospel of the day.

The Second Lesson (Romans 16:25-27) is the doxology and conclusion of the present Letter to the Romans. While the best manuscript tradition has this text in this place, other important witnesses have it at the end of chapter 14 or the end of chapter 15 or omit it altogether. It may best be understood as a deutero-Pauline addition to the text, appended in the circulation of Romans among the churches and having a varied history in the tradition. The language of hidden and revealed mystery, indeed, recalls most vividly the language of Colossians (1:26; 2:2; 4:3) and Ephesians (3:1-10), books widely regarded as deutero-Pauline. As in those texts, the revelation of the mystery is linked to the preaching and ministry of Paul himself. Here, that revelation is also linked to the disclosure of the old Scriptures in the present time (cf. Rom. 15:4).

The text is a wonderful coda to Romans. The preaching of the gospel of Jesus Christ is the ancient secret now made known and is the meaning of the Scriptures. This gospel results in the strengthening of the community and brings about faith. This is not faith that results in obedience; it is the faith that obeys by being faith, by trusting the word that has been heard. And this preaching and strengthening and trusting take place in the context of praise to God: The community itself gives glory to God through the Christ of the gospel in its midst.

Read next to the other texts for the day, this doxological coda to Romans becomes a verbal image of the liturgical assembly. The prophetic scriptures disclosed are the royal oracles transformed and proclaimed anew by Gabriel to us today. Paul's preaching of the gospel becomes the task of the current assembly's preacher, interpreting the prophetic and apostolic texts. This complex "word" comes to strengthen the assembly. It comes as a revelation of light in the midst of the darkness of Advent. Hearing this word, the community is enabled to believe, like Mary who is the type of "the obedience of faith." Hearing this word, the assembly is formed into praise to God through Christ. It does the *eucharistia* of the table. Such an assembly is the house and temple of God.

AROUND THE TEXTS

One of the marks of current liturgical change has been the recovery of *blue* as a possible color for Advent. This change has much to recommend it. For one thing, the use of purple (the more common liturgical color) seems to bring congregations to regard Advent as a kind of Lent for Christmas, a fast and a penitential time that prepares for the feast. While this may have been a useful observance at one time, it seems unlikely to succeed today. We have suggested already that Advent is best understood as having its own integrity as a Christian response to the solstice-time.

For another thing, blue receives the darkness of the time into the vesture of the church, but receives it with a subtle transformation. Blue is the color of a *bright* night, of the sky just before morning. Blue receives the darkness and suggests the dawning light.

And for another thing, blue is the color of Mary. The congregation, in its assembly for Word and Sacrament, is clothed in the color that has been classically associated with the great woman of faith.

It is widely understood that Mary may serve as a "type" of the church. Luther, in his commentary on the Magnificat, proposed Mary as the example for the believing Christian of one who trusts in the word of God against all appearances. But such use of "type" and "example" should be adopted with care. The point is not that Advent is a good time to think about Mary's pregnancy, about details of her impregnation or labor or childbirth. There is nothing in the Bible to help with that. Such a focus will draw us away from an authentic use of Advent. Nor ought we find that the accent should fall on Mary's "receptivity." Such an understanding of Mary's role frequently is paired with an understanding of the "good" role of women—or of Christians generally—as being passive. Behind such reflections there hovers the history of an ancient biology that regarded women as being wholly passive participants in conception, providing no ovum but only a matrix for the male seed to grow, only the "matter" for the male "form."

The Mary of our text is active, both in doubting questions and in the response of faith. We have said here that the nature of her child and of the gift of God transforms her doubt and enables her faith, her response to the Word. In her response, we may say the Holy Spirit has already overshadowed her, creating faith. In her song she proclaims a vigorous— and wholly untimorous—image of the activity of God in the world. But she does not simply see this activity and "ponder" it. She proclaims it.

Then let the color of the assembly in Advent be blue. The light is dawning. The Spirit is active in the assembly, enlivening the Word. We all together, men and women, may join in the faithful, courageous, and active assenting and proclaiming that we see in the mother of God.

The Nativity of Our Lord, 1
The Service at Night

Lutheran	Roman Catholic	Episcopal	Common Lectionary
Isa. 9:2-7	Isa. 9:2-7	Isa. 9:2-4, 6-7	Isa. 9:2-7
Titus 2:11-14	Titus 2:11-14	Titus 2:11-14	Titus 2:11-14
Luke 2:1-20	Luke 2:1-14	Luke 2:1-14	Luke 2:1-20

ABOUT THE TEXTS

The pericopes appointed for Christmas Day, in all the current adaptations of the new lectionary, include three full sets of texts. These three sets arise from the fifth-century custom of emphasizing the importance of the festival by celebrating three different liturgies, each with its own Propers, through the course of its hours. In Rome, and then in the churches dependent on Rome, there was a liturgy in the midst of the night, a liturgy at dawn, and a liturgy in the full day.

Since the evening and the night were already regarded—as in Jewish timekeeping—as the beginning of day, the liturgy in the evening or at midnight was considered the first liturgy of Christmas. This night service used the Lukan infancy narrative and the Isaian royal oracle with its theme of light in darkness. It celebrated the birth of Christ as the coming of God's light into our night.

Then there was a liturgy at dawn, the rising sun being especially important on this solstice day. Called the "mass of the shepherds," it used the account of those who came to the manger (Luke 2:15-20) as an invitation to the assembly to know Christ and to share in the proclamation of the message in the world.

The primary liturgy of the day, to which the other gatherings served as prelude, was the third liturgy. It included the prologue to John as the great Gospel of the incarnation and as the central reading of the day. "The true light that enlightens everyone has come into the world," this reading proclaimed, giving new meaning to the full light of this midwinter day. The threefold celebration thus used the passage of the day from darkness to light as a frame for its proclamation of the Christian meaning of solstice.

The current lectionaries include adaptations of the same three lists of texts, but it is likely that the old "mass of the shepherds" list is the one least used. In any case, because of the importance of liturgy on both Christmas Eve and Christmas morning in current practice, this volume will include commentaries on the other two lists, the ones historically appointed to the night and to the full day. These are the lists included in the *Lutheran Book of Worship* as numbers 1 and 2, in the Roman Catholic *Ordo Lectionum* as *in nocte* and *in die,* in the *Book of Common Prayer* as Christmas Day I and Christmas Day III, and in the Common Lectionary as First Proper and Third Proper.*

The Gospel (Luke 2:1-20) appointed in the tradition for the liturgy at midnight or the liturgy that is on "Christmas Eve" is the Lukan birth narrative. In fact, the very terms and language of this narrative have become so familiar, so woven into the ritual pattern of people's observance of Christmas, as to make the pericope less a text for interpretation than itself a multivalent symbol, an ornament or a gem hung in the Christmas setting, an evocation of memories from past Christmases.

---

*A current ecumenical proposal has suggested a way to unify these lists and maintain the centrality of the Johannine prologue to the feast. In congregations where the vast majority of people come to church only on "Christmas Eve," that is, to the Christmas Day Eucharist that is held in the night, the liturgy might *begin* with a reading of the Lucan nativity (Luke 2:1-14 or 2:1-20). There could follow a procession—perhaps a procession to the creche or the tree—followed by the Gloria and the opening prayer. The Gospel of the liturgy proper, then, would be John 1:1-14. The analogy to this arrangement is the pattern of reading on Passion Sunday, when the narrative of the entrance into Jerusalem is read as the "processional Gospel" and the Passion account as the Gospel of the day. The proposal itself, whether or not it is widely followed, has the merit of calling our attention again to the importance of the Johannine themes, rather than the birth narratives, for the central meaning of the feast.

Such a symbolic use of the reading is not entirely inconsistent with what seems to be the intention of the text itself. The text is full of symbols: Bethlehem, house of David, the angels, and, in thick succession, the royal titles *Savior, Messiah,* and *Lord.* These symbols are set amidst counter-symbols: Caesar Augustus, the decree, the census for taxation. We read these words wrongly if we take them to be the diary of historical events. It is, rather, as if we are gently asked which reign is more important for "all the world" (*pasan tēn oikoumenēn,* 2:1), the decrees of Augustus or the birth of the Davidic Messiah. Here Jesus' identity is strongly asserted through Davidic symbols, the royal meaning of which has been so carefully prepared and nuanced in the first chapter of the Gospel (see above on the Gospel for the Fourth Sunday in Advent).

Here also we are assured, in a manner characteristic for Luke, that the birth of this Messiah occurs in the midst of obedience by Galileans to a Roman edict, not in rebellion: The only historic Roman census of Judea we know of from secular sources was the one under Quirinius that occasioned the great revolt of Judas the Galilean, the founder of the Zealots. Here is a child, born in peace, surrounded by signs of the Davidic dignity and by the angel-proclaimed word of God. And here is the edict of the emperor and the memory of violence. The text is itself a symbol and a dialectic of symbols.

Then, when the identity of Jesus has been set out symbolically, we are given models for possible reception of the symbols. We may proclaim them in thanksgiving with the shepherds (2:17, 20). We may wonder with "all who heard it" (2:18). We may contemplatively ponder them with Mary who "kept all these things . . . in her heart" (2:19). The text is a symbol intended to be set in the context of the assembly of faith. The iconic use of the pericope on Christmas Eve, as if the text were a symbol inviting us into participation with the thing symbolized, is prepared for by the use of the nativity narrative in the Book of Luke itself.

But we may be helped to a fresh and surprising reading of the text—and the preacher of the evening may be helped to fresh proclamation of the Christmas mystery—if we realize that there remain many unanswered questions about the use and meaning of some of the symbols of the text. For example, why does this account make use of *shepherds*? Are they representatives of the poor and despised of the world, of the sinners with whom the Jesus of the Lukan Gospel will associate? Are they placed here in order to anticipate what follows in that Gospel and to contrast the angel's message *to* the poor with the imperial edict worked by governors *on* the poor? Or, are they rustics, used in many Hellenistic texts as the witnesses and participants in divine-human births? Do they function to alert the Greek reader that something divine is going on here, that this child is "son of

God" in more than just the old royal sense? Or, are they biblical imagery? In the Scriptures, "shepherding" is a way of describing kingly rule (cf. Ezek. 34:2). David is a shepherd, from among shepherds. At last, God is the one who will take over the shepherding (Ezek. 34:11-12). Are the shepherds present to alert us, like Bethlehem itself, to the Davidic messiah who is now the presence of God's own shepherding (Ezek. 34:23)? Or, are all three of these possibilities correct?

And what is the meaning of the angelic song? Is the promise of peace a promise which includes all humankind, among all of whom God's merciful goodwill is to be active? Or is it a promise to "the elect," the remnant, the ones chosen by the good pleasure of God? And, if the latter, how does that song relate to the intention of the text in locating the event in "all the world"? Does the Lukan text take an earlier Christian song, in which the idea of the remnant functioned, and transform its meaning in the new context of the "whole inhabited world" (*oikoumenē*, 2:1)? If "among human beings of God's good will" is the best attested reading, was the widespread reading "on earth peace, among human beings God's good will" a change that was made in the later use of Luke that legitimately reflects a new meaning for an old song when used in this nativity context?

And what of the "inn" (*katalyma*, 2:7) in which there is no place, and the "manger" (*phatnē*, 2:7, 12, 16) in which Jesus is laid (*aneklinen*, 2:7)? What do they mean? Are they the materials of poverty, contrasting again with the emperor? Is this an anticipation of Luke 9:58: "the Son of Man has nowhere to lay his head"? Or are they also biblical imagery? Raymond Brown (*The Birth of the Messiah* [Garden City, N.Y.: Doubleday, 1977], 418–20) has made the fine suggestion that behind our text there stands the Greek translation Luke would have known of Jer. 14:8 and of Isa. 1:3. Jeremiah pleads: "O hope of Isael, its savior in time of trouble, why should you be like a stranger in the land, like a wayfarer who turns aside to tarry for a night" (LXX: "who turns aside to an inn," *ekklinōn eis katalyma*). Here, in the Lukan text, there is a savior (cf. Luke 2:11) who does not turn aside, is not a stranger, but is laid down among the people in their trouble. And Isaiah laments: "The ox knows its owner, and the ass its master's crib" (LXX: "the manger of its Lord," *tēn phatnēn tou kyriou autou*); "but Israel does not know, my people does not understand." But here, in the Lukan text, there is a *Lord* (cf. Luke 2:11) whom Israel may know when the nation comes, in the shepherds, to the manger. Here is the place where Israel may find joy, true food, and the presence of God. Israel, by the mercy of God, has begun to know the manger of its Lord.

It is no wonder, then, that hymnody and iconography have made the place of the manger to be a stable and have placed in the stable an ox and an ass. Biblical motifs have operated in that imagery just as they have in the tradition that places Mary on a donkey as she rides to Bethlehem. In the stable is the sign of the reversal of Isa. 1:3. With the donkey, Zech. 9:9 is applied to Mary's child: "Rejoice greatly, O daughter of Zion . . . your king comes . . . humble and riding on an ass." Only now the "daughter of Zion" herself rides, bearing the child who is the humble king.

The Lukan nativity story is rightly seen as an icon, an integral symbol of the identity of Jesus in our midst. It is also rightly discovered to be mysterious, refreshing us with new insights and new questions.

Read in the night of the Christmas feast, the text may flash with light from these and from many more of its facets. The identity of the one who is present with us is proclaimed. He is a "king" unlike Caesar but also unlike the Davidic kings. His bed is with the poor in their need. His presence now, in this assembly, introduces us to singing to God with the angels and proclaiming thanksgiving to God with the shepherds: In Jesus the community is restored to the praise of God. The Word that occurs here, in texts and preaching and sacrament, is also for our hearts, to be kept and pondered. And here, at this table, we may come to know God, like a donkey that knows where to eat, and knows the manger of its Lord.

But the principal facets of the text that shine forth when it is read in assembly this night are those that deal with the theme of light. The shepherds who watch—whether they are signs of the poor, of the divine birth, or of the Davidic kingship—watch "by night." When the angel appears, the glory of the Lord "shines." Read on the night that was anciently regarded as the solstice itself, the darkness of the shepherds gathers up all our Advent waiting, together with all the waiting of Israel, all the need of the poor, and all the ignorance of religion itself. And the shining surrounds the Word and Sacrament here, which proclaim also to us the message of the angel.

The First Lesson (Isaiah 9:2-7) for this night is a text from First Isaiah. It is probably to be regarded as an oracle spoken at the accession of an ancient, unnamed Judean king. The oracle then came to be included in the prophetic collection of Isaian oracles. Perhaps it even came to be read out at all enthronements. Spoken of a Davidic king (v. 7), claiming the promise to David known in the tradition of royal ideology (cf. Psalm 89; 2 Samuel 7), this oracle asserts the great gifts that come with the king, according to the hope of that ideology. With this enthronement come light in darkness, joy in sorrow, the end of captivity to foreign rule, the end of invasions and burning villages, and a peaceful and unending rule.

The "child" that is born, the "son" that is given (v. 6), is none other than the king himself, who is "born" as "son of the god" (Pss. 2:7; 89:26-27) when he is made king. This widespread feature of oriental monarchy—

that becoming king is becoming son of the god—goes paired with another: The king is given new royal epithets (v. 6). At least one of these names strains to the breaking point the ability of orthodox Israelite faith to live peacefully with such monarchy: The king is called "Mighty God." The rationale of such titles lay probably in poetic extension from the title "son of God." If the monarch is God's "son," he may also be called by God's names. Some prophets of the Israelite tradition would find this extension appalling. It is one small evidence of the ways in which monarchy continually teetered on the edge of idolatry and apostasy in trying to adapt religious material from the surrounding world to both the faith and the current need of Israel. Oracles full of royal prerogatives, an endless reign, and divine names for the monarch are drawn from that surrounding religious culture.

But such a description was never fulfilled by any king, in Judah or in Israel. The text itself is full of an excess of hope and a fervent desire for peace, spilling out of the historical limits of the text's origin, reaching from a history of agony ("every boot of the tramping warrior . . . every garment rolled in blood," 9:5) toward a hope beyond the ability of any monarchy. That excess comes to be used tonight. Read at Christmas, the old hope in kings is criticized and transformed. The celebration is now around a birth, not an enthronement. In this child—one speaks now of a real human child, not a monarch described in metaphor—God acts to give what royal actions could never give: peace, joy, real light, God's own presence. Read next to the Lukan infancy account, this text heightens the contrast in Luke between Jesus and the emperor, between Jesus and the Davidic kings. Its opening words—"The people who walked in darkness have seen a great light"—also serve to draw our attention to the night of the shepherds and the shining of the angelic glory. We thereby see the outlines of the Christian solstice: In Christ, God's glory dawns in the night of our need.

The Second Lesson (Titus 2:11-14) is a text from the pastoral epistles inviting the readers to see the manifestation of God's grace in the world. This manifestation forms a people who live lives turned toward the final epiphany of God and Christ. Such a people is a "chosen people," redeemed by Christ. Read on Christmas, the "epiphanies" of the text all come to be focused on the light that shines forth tonight. Here is the appearing of the grace of God for the salvation of all. Here, in this assembly, is a "chosen people" who turn toward that appearing and bear witness to its intention of mercy toward all people. The "appearing" of the Titus letter, the light in darkness of the Isaian oracle, the shining around the angel's announcement at night, the manger of Israel's Lord, and the Word and Sacraments that give life to this assembly—all these things interpenetrate each other and give light to our night.

AROUND THE TEXTS

The proper chants of this night's liturgy receive and greet the texts as if we were the shepherds hearing the message of the angel, as if the texts themselves were the presence of the child. "To you is born this day a Savior, Christ the Lord," we may sing in either the responsorial psalm (Roman) or the verse (Lutheran). This assembly has become the locus of the shining Word of God. The prayer of the day celebrates that shining even more strongly, giving the classic meaning of the Christian adaptation of the winter solstice: "Almighty God, you made this holy night shine with the brightness of the true Light. Grant that as we have known on earth the mysteries of that Light, we may also come to the fulness of his joys in heaven." The light that is present this night also draws us beyond this night; the tangibility of God's mercy draws us toward God beyond our experience, into the mystery of the Trinity. So the Preface prays, at the table of the tangible and visible word: "In the wonder and mystery of the Word made flesh you have opened the eyes of faith to a new and radiant vision of your glory; that, beholding the God made visible, we may be drawn to love the God whom we cannot see."

Of the symbols that we see tonight, the strongest—besides the pericopes and the eucharistic bread and wine themselves—may be the tree. In churches that observe the Advent simplicity, keeping a lighted tree absent from liturgical space until this night, the sudden presence of the tree is a powerful thing. Now a burning tree, a light-tree, stands near these texts, in the room of the eucharistic table, and its presence lends an interpretation to the church's Word and Sacrament.

Trees have, of course, long functioned as cosmic symbols. A single tree may be, like Yggdrasil in Norse myth, a sign of the unity of all things, of the universe as one. A lighted tree, an evergreen tree burning with candles or white lights, may be like the sun hoped for by the ancients, illuminating all things and holding all things in unity and green fertility. We set out gifts under such trees in our homes, as if we could thereby partake in that abundance which the restored sun may renew in the earth. Such a tree is a sun symbol—now the full burning sun connected to all things, not the growing sun-orb of the Advent wreath.

But when set next to Word and Sacrament, this sun has become the "Sun of Righteousness." The light of the tree emphasizes the solstice imagery of this celebration: the light of the texts—shining in the darkness (First Lesson), appearing as grace and glory (Second Lesson), shining in the angelic message in the night (Gospel)—and the light of God made visible in the Eucharist. The tree itself is thereby reinterpreted, pointing beyond itself in the way that the whole Christmas observance points beyond itself. Christ present in our midst burns with the light of God. Christ in our midst is fruitfulness and abundance for all peoples. Christ—who imposes no imperial unity, but lies with the poor in birth as in death—is our only hope for the true unity of all things. Christ is our light and sun and tree, in all seasons. The tree is a symbol of Christ without, for instance, our ever hanging monograms of Christ's name on its branches. Set in our room of assembly on this dark night it carries our current solstice hopes into that room and sets them next to the Word of God. According to the imagery of faith, a tree of light and abundance is what we meet whenever we encounter the cross, coming with all nations to make nests in Christ's branches or to feast on his life-giving fruits. Tonight and throughout the twelve days of Christmas we make that imagery visible, using the culture's Christmas tree yet transforming it as well.

The Nativity of Our Lord, 2
The Service in the Day

Lutheran	Roman Catholic	Episcopal	Common Lectionary
Isa. 52:7-10	Isa. 52:7-10	Isa. 52:7-10	Isa. 52:7-10
Heb. 1:1-9	Heb. 1:1-6	Heb. 1:1-12	Heb. 1:1-12
John 1:1-14	John 1:1-18	John 1:1-14	John 1:1-14

ABOUT THE TEXTS

The Gospel (John 1:1-14) for the principal service of Christmas, the liturgy of Christmas morning, is the Johannine prologue. This text is the fullest New Testament celebration of the identity of Jesus as God incarnate. According to the text, to encounter Jesus Christ with faith, naming him truly in spite of his hiddenness in the darkness of the world's rejection and of his death, is to encounter the light of God. To so meet him is to come to the life of God, to the power that makes us "children of God," to the Word and wisdom of God, to the fullness of the grace and truth and glory of God. To so "behold" and "receive" him is not only to encounter the

Word which creates and sustains all things but to encounter the very disclosure of God's own self. The fullness of the terms of the text, heaped
up and recurring, is an image of the fullness of that disclosure of God in
Christ's flesh. The richness of the text in our ears is a tangible enactment
of the "fulness we all receive."

It is not wrong to call the text a "celebration." In fact, current scholarly
opinion is largely united in regarding most of the prologue as having come
from a communal liturgical *hymn* (perhaps 1:1-5, 10-12, 14, 16), very
much like the later hymns that have been preserved as the second-century
"Odes of Solomon." The widely shared supposition is that the author or
editor of the Fourth Gospel knew this hymn and used it, interweaving in
it the material about John the Baptist (1:6-9, 15) and other explanatory
phrases (1:13, 17-18) and thereby making it the beginning of a book. The
community that sang such a hymn would have been able to use that mix
of language—Hellenistic philosophical and religious terms combined with
the biblical tradition—which later would give rise both to Gnosticism and
to Christian creedal orthodoxy. The purpose here, however, was not philosophical or doctrinal. As a hymn, the purpose of the text was praise. As
prologue, the purpose was to begin the Gospel. In both cases—in the midst
of the praise of the community and in the very words of the Gospel read
in the community—the one who is life and light is beheld in faith (cf.
20:29-31) and received.

We have already noted (see above on the Gospel for the Third Sunday
in Advent) how the "beginning" (*archē*, Mark 1:1) of the second Gospel
became the cosmic beginning of John 1:1. In John the word *archē* evokes
the beginning of all things in the biblical tradition and the very first words
of the Scriptures themselves: "In the beginning God . . ." (Gen. 1:1). We
can imagine the author or the final editor of the Fourth Gospel working
with the book of Mark. Perhaps the opening Markan word evoked the use
of the communal hymn which, placed at the outset of the book, was meant
to evoke the first words of Genesis and, thereby, the whole force of the
Scripture.

But this cosmic and scriptural beginning is still the beginning of the
"gospel"—in both senses—the beginning of the testimony to the light and
of the book that represents that testimony. Just as in Mark, the first thing,
the ground of the gospel, is the Word of God. Here, however, that Word
is not a prophetic quotation (Mark 1:2-3) but the very wisdom of God
which came to dwell in Israel and to speak in all the prophets (John 1:10).
Just as in Mark, the Baptist is united with that beginning and made a
witness of the present force of that Word. However, here his witness is
interwoven with the hymn about the Word, the hymn that brings in itself

all the force of Scripture, instead of being interwoven with specific prophetic quotations.

The hymn is the beginning of the gospel. That is, it envisions an assembly and is aimed at a present event. The prologue says what will take place in proclaiming the contents of the book in the community: God will be known among those who receive the incarnate Word, believe in his name, behold his glory, receive from his fullness.

The hymn is the beginning of the gospel. That is, the things that are said in this text are said of Jesus Christ, in order to speak Jesus Christ in the assembly. It may be that the original hymn proclaimed the Word present with God before creation (1:1-2), then the Word through whom creation occurred (1:3-4), then the Word present as light and wisdom in Israel (1:5, 10-12), then the Word incarnate (1:14), and then the present community's share in the Word (1:16). But when John the Baptist's witness is placed between v. 5 and v. 10, at least the paragraph following (vv. 10-13) is made to speak of the historic Jesus Christ: He is the one in the world, the one not known (cf. 1:26, "among you stands one whom you do not know") and not received. That is, he is the Word and wisdom in Israel, the very content of the prophetic Scriptures.

This reading suggests that the light that "shines in the darkness, and the darkness has not overcome it" (v. 5) is also Jesus Christ, crucified and risen. The interest of this Gospel is not in speculation about "the pre-existent Word." Such time categories, important in later theological speculation, do not matter here. Rather, Jesus Christ, whom the community encounters and from whom the community receives, is proclaimed here as all that the first paragraph (vv. 1-4) has to say. The Fourth Gospel can say that Jesus is before John (cf. v. 15: "John bore witness to him, and cried, "This was he of whom I said, '. . . he was before me' "), and it can enact that priority by putting Christ in vv. 1-5 before John the Baptist in vv. 6-9. For the prologue, if not for the hymn, Jesus Christ is the very Word with God, the Word that is the content of all the Scriptures beginning at Genesis 1:1, the Word that creates all things, the Word which *is* God. By the insertion of John the Baptist, what may have been a speculative hymn or a Hellenistic way of enunciating salvation history has been turned into a present proclamation of the meaning of the crucified and risen one. John's name in v. 6 prepares us to hear Jesus' name in v. 17, now as the deeper meaning of the Scriptures, over against the Scriptures as simply being the law. That name at the end is not, as the hymn is used in the prologue, the final entry in a series of visits by the Word. The name of the one whom the community encounters gathers to itself all the meanings of the whole hymn.

But then the centrality of the verse about the incarnation (v. 14) is underscored. All the meanings of the hymn—the word of creation, wisdom in Israel, light in the darkness—are "beheld" in the Word made flesh, that is, in the Word made encounterable as a human person. The Word "dwells among us," "tents among us" (*eskēnōsen en hēmin*) as God dwells in Israel, tabernacles among the people, and promises at last to dwell among humankind. And the congregation gathers around that "dwelling," beholding and receiving the fullness of grace and truth.

Read at Christmas, it is of course this verse 14 of the text that is heard loudest. But just as the feast should not be misunderstood as a "birthday" of Jesus, this text ought not be misused as an account of the day when the Word became flesh. Today is solstice time, the old festival when there was hope for the presence of fruitfulness and summer fullness in the land. The liturgy proclaims that all the fullness of God—light, life, grace, truth, the meaning of the Scriptures, the Word that holds all things together—is encountered now in "beholding" Jesus Christ. And Christ is beheld as dwelling in the assembly in the Word and table which are set out on this Christmas morning.

It is solstice time. The light of a brief winter day is full and bright now. The liturgy proclaims that the light that gives life and shines in all darkness is in our midst, illuminating with glory much more than our winter days. It is new year's time, a time for new beginnings, and with this prologue we "begin" the gospel again. We begin both senses of the word "gospel": We start to read through the Fourth Gospel book, which will function as a pericope source, especially at festivals, throughout this year. We also hope once again to found our community in Christ proclaimed here so that we may know God. We begin in the Word of God encountered in Christ, and all cosmic beginnings are pulled into that encounter.

The First Lesson (Isaiah 52:7-10) is a text from Second Isaiah celebrating the expected return of the exiles to Jerusalem. This return is proclaimed as if a new reign were being announced, not of any king but of God. The message of the runners becomes a kind of enthronement oracle. It is also announced as if *God*—and not just the exiles—were coming home to Jerusalem. The watchers, the city, and finally all the nations behold God coming to the city. The temple, which has been deserted, will be inhabited again.

Read on Christmas, the good news of the runners becomes the Christmas gospel, the joy of the city becomes Christmas rejoicing, and the visible coming of God becomes the incarnation. Second Isaiah's hope for the city is seen to be a living word, inviting the waste place of the world to rejoice in the comfort of God.

Read next to the Gospel of the day, the text underscores the accent of the Johannine prologue on light and on beholding. "The word became flesh and dwelt among us . . . we have beheld his glory," proclaims the prologue. "With their own eyes they see the return of the LORD to Zion," proclaims the prophet. The theme is repeated and universalized: "Before the eyes of all the nations" God acts, and "all the ends of the earth shall see the salvation of our God." We are invited to be the nations beholding God's salvation, seeing God come to dwell among humanity, by beholding in faith the flesh of Christ who dwells in our midst in Word and table. This is the light we may see returning in full radiance this solstice, a light intended for all nations and for the comfort of all the wretched more surely than is the sun.

The Second Lesson (Hebrews 1:1-9) is the opening verses of the Letter to the Hebrews. This letter, written in a Hellenistic Jewish-Christian milieu much like that of the Johannine community, shows in these initial verses a remarkable similarity—perhaps even a dependence upon—the themes of the Johannine prologue. The themes are worked out quite differently, but when the first chapter of Hebrews is read side by side with the Gospel of this day we note this in both: The word or speech of God is central; the "son" is that speech; all things have been created through him; he shows forth the glory of God and shares God's "nature." What is added in the Hebrews letter is a lengthy application of ancient material from royal enthronements (Pss. 2:7; 45:6-7) to Jesus. Then the title "son" is seen against its original background, the royal titles in Israel, but it is also seen to propose something greater: The one who reigns now is not a new king but Jesus. This "son" is God's own final word, the showing forth of God's own glory and nature.

Read next to the Gospel of the day, the text serves to accentuate the very themes that are important to the feast. Here in our midst is the Word which creates and upholds all things. Here is the glory of God. But the text also serves the classic intention of epistle readings. It symbolizes the church gathered around the central readings of the day. This word of God is spoken to *us* in the Son. This assembly is the place of the speaking.

AROUND THE TEXTS

Much of the hymnody of Christmas has the sense of an old antiphon, classically sung at the Magnificat of Evening Prayer on Christmas Day: *Hodie Christus natus est,* "Today Christ is born; today salvation has appeared. Today the just exult and say, Glory to God in the highest. Alleluia." So we sing solemnly in the church: "Yea, Lord, we greet thee, born this happy morning." Or, more popularly, we sing the carol: "Give ye heed to what we say; Jesus Christ is born today."

This theme of the *hodie,* the "today" of Christian poetry, is liable to misunderstanding. It can be taken to mean that we receive Christ as a kind of nature god: He is born at winter solstice like the sun; he is crucified and risen in springtime, like the vegetation. "Jesus Christ" then becomes only a name for our own experience of the year. It can also be taken to be simply poetic excess: We pretend it is the ancient birthday and so sing to the birthday child.

But the *hodie* of the liturgy means something else, something deeper. In the assembly the events of the Scripture address us today. And in any facet of those events, we meet the whole. We have seen this already in the prologue of John. All the "history" of the word and wisdom of God is encountered in Jesus Christ. Indeed, God is known in Christ. And Christ is encountered as "we all receive, grace upon grace." This encounter connects us to the need of the world and holds us before the face of God.

In church, the story of the birth is read, but so is the prologue to John. So is the old story of the hope of exiles, mirroring agonies and hopes in the whole world today. Then the meal is held—the "mass" in Christ*mas*— proclaiming the whole Christ, especially his death and resurrection, and encountering him now. It is not that we are reenacting the birth story, but that the original story itself was meant to be proclaimed as gospel in the present, to draw us into the present encounter with the mercy of God in Christ. And the church has found it pastorally useful to set out this particular way into the whole gospel in the dark time of year, using the name "Jesus Christ" to address and transform our experience of time.

Today, in the assembly, salvation has appeared. Today, in the Word read and preached here we meet the birth of Christ for us, we meet the presence of the richness of grace in the world. Today we meet the tangibility of that grace, even in the midst of hunger and death, as this life-giving meal. Today light shines in the darkness, manifesting itself as the Word that holds all things together. Today we sing with the angels, enabled to find words that speak to God in praise. Among those words are a great variety of carols and hymns that speak this *today.* Their variety and richness echo the "fullness" from which we all receive grace upon grace.

The First Sunday after Christmas

Lutheran	Roman Catholic	Episcopal	Common Lectionary
Isa. 45:22-25	Gen. 15:1-6; 21:1-3	Isa. 61:10—62:3	Isa. 61:10—62:3
Col. 3:12-17	Heb. 11:8, 11-12, 17-19	Gal. 3:23-25; 4:4-7	Gal. 4:4-7
Luke 2:25-40	Luke 2:22-40	John 1:1-18	Luke 2:22-40

ABOUT THE TEXTS

The Gospel (Luke 2:25-40) for this day, in all but Episcopal use, is the account of the presentation of Jesus in the temple. This text is also read on the Feast of the Presentation or Candlemas (February 2), forty days after Christmas, as a final echo of the Christmas cycle. That feast at forty days is an image as well of the forty days from birth that the law required for the purification of the mother of a male child (Lev. 12:2-4). Such a counting of days was probably undertaken in order to enable a Christian countercelebration to the pagan observance of the February fertility feast, Lupercalia. But when the text is read in the days of Christmas the intention is different. Here we are not waiting the forty days, acting out the drama. Rather, the text is used to proclaim again the light-theme of the Christian solstice and, at the same time, to connect the mystery of Christmas to the mystery of the Passion of Christ.

Light and suffering are the themes of the text itself. A pair of human couples is set out to frame the content of the text: Mary and Joseph bring the child. Simeon and Anna receive him. A remarkable setting is provided: The temple is the place of powerful religious events for Israel. Then, in the midst of these couples and on the site of this temple, Jesus is proclaimed as the light of God and shown forth as one who is opposed, as the stone of stumbling and of building.

The temple suggests the theme of suffering; after all, the parents come with animals to be killed. Luke, somewhat inaccurately according to the law but strongly to the point of the text, suggests that these animals are to be killed in the stead of the child and that such "redemption" is also the parents' "purification." In fact, the law required five shekels as the redemption price of the firstborn male (Num. 18:16) and a lamb and a dove or two doves as the ritual cleansing of the mother (Lev. 12:6-7). These traditions are conflated here, the birds for the sacrifice being juxtaposed to the "presented" child. Indeed, a temple is a place of ritual killing. That the child is carried into that place makes us hear the text in a certain way. In succeeding texts in the Gospel of Luke, Jesus will be spoken against in the temple (Luke 20:1ff.) and his death will be prophesied there (20:15; cf. 19:47). If he is "set" (2:34) for the falling and rising of many in Israel, it is as a stone in temple building (20:17-18), which is rejected and yet becomes the source and ground of the rising new temple. He falls and rises and so is the source of all rising. If, as a firstborn male, he is "devoted to the Lord" (2:23; cf. Exod. 34:20) and only redeemed by the doves, Simeon's speech makes clear that he is not redeemed for long. Although the words about a sword piercing Mary's soul are not clear and have been the source of endless interpretations, Simeon's speech in the temple makes clear that she too is to suffer. The Gospel of the day sets suffering in the midst of Christmas.

But the temple also suggests the theme of light. This house is, after all, the ancient dwelling place of the glory of God. It symbolizes God's covenant intention to dwell in the midst of the people, being their God, wiping away tears, and showing forth salvation to all the earth. The temple setting, then, makes more brilliant Simeon's words in greeting the light and glory of God in this child. It makes stronger the frame around this light—Simeon's expectation of the consolation of Israel before and Anna's speaking to those expecting the redemption of Jerusalem after. That consolation and redemption come to the temple. And just as Isaiah promises, they come there—to Jerusalem and to the temple—in the sight of all the nations (Luke 2:31-32; cf. Isa. 52:10). The temple of which this child is the cornerstone is not a place of killing. His suffering is the end of that. It is the dwelling place of God. It is the place of light.

Simeon's two speeches carry these themes. The first praises the light (2:29-32); the second announces the suffering (2:34-35). In some ways the acceptance of death present in the first prepares us to hear the pain of the second. But the text does not leave it there. Anna comes. She, not Simeon, has the last word, speaking like another "Anna," Hannah, who sang of the consolations of God (1 Sam. 2:1-10). She is old, as near death as Simeon; she carries in herself all the possibilities of suffering. Her summarizing theme, however, is not death, but thanksgiving to God and proclamation of the presence of the child. In thanksgiving and proclamation the thesis of light and the antithesis of suffering have their synthesis.

There are hidden themes in the text as well. The parents bring an offering as it is prescribed in the law: "a pair of turtledoves, or two young pigeons." What is not said is that this is the offering of the poor: "She shall bring to the priest . . . a lamb . . . and a pigeon. . . . And if she cannot afford a lamb, then she shall take two turtledoves or two young pigeons" (Lev. 12:6-8; cf. 5:7). Does this poverty carry on the contrast with imperial Rome and with the Davidic kings begun in the nativity story? Is the lamb for the offering the child himself? And there is this: The event of the text occurs in the temple, but it has little to do with the rites of the temple themselves except as they provide a frame. Although Christian iconography regularly presents Simeon as a priest, nothing in the text suggests this. It is Anna who is associated with the temple, dwelling there in her piety. But as a woman she has access neither to the center of the temple nor to its rites. The entire exchange of the text takes place in the temple, but it seems hidden there. The child is given no priestly or institutional attention. The rituals go on in disregard for this presence of the light just as they go on in disregard for the poor.

But then how is it that "all peoples" see the salvation of God? Because we see it. When the text is read, the concrete approachability of the child is present here. The Holy Spirit that enlivens this assembly invites us to sing with Simeon of the light and the suffering. The song of Simeon is used in some churches as an apt post-communion hymn, sung when we have taken the body of Christ into our own hands. In any case, the sure Word of God and the table of the Lord form us, with Anna, to give thanks through Christ to God. We are invited to see that the presence of Christ with the poor is more important than all sacrifices and temple rituals. This assembly becomes the place of the central event of this text.

Read on the first Sunday to occur in the twelve days of the Christmas feast, this pericope continues to celebrate that the light for which the world hopes is present, dwelling in the midst of humankind in the hidden child. By interweaving the themes of light and the Passion and by associating them with Anna's temple thanksgiving, the mystery of Christmas draws us into the mystery of the cross and resurrection and into the present reality of a community of thanksgiving in Christ.

The Gospel read in Episcopal churches on this day is the full Johannine prologue (see above on the Gospel for the Christmas Service in the Day). The intention is to proclaim this central text on the Sunday within the feast, especially since many people may have only heard the Lukan nativity on Christmas day itself. What is more, the final verses of the prologue (vv. 15-18) have the effect of carrying on the celebration through the twelve days: from the fullness of the incarnate Word we all receive, grace upon grace (John 1:16).

The First Lesson (Isaiah 45:22-25), in Lutheran use, is an Isaian text that speaks out the sure word of God that all nations, all the ends of the earth, shall turn to the God who is in the midst of Israel. Its intention on this day is to underscore the Isaian themes we hear in the song of Simeon.

The reading in the Episcopal lectionary and the Common Lectionary is *Isa. 61:10—62:3,* a lesson that was read in part by the other lectionaries on the Third Sunday in Advent (see above), the old Sunday of rejoicing. The intention here is to let this Isaiah text lead us into festival rejoicing at Christmas, rejoicing in the redemption of the earth itself.

The Roman lectionary is determined by the decision to call this First Sunday after Christmas by a new name: the Feast of the Holy Family. The First Lesson here is *Gen. 15:1-6* and *21:1-3*. This reading proposes Abraham, Sarah, and their child Isaac, as another example of a couple with an unexpected child. Such a pairing of the birth of Isaac with the birth of Jesus is intended to speak of the presence of grace and mercy in the world, the major theme of the entire twelve days. The accent is placed on the child as the surprising child of promise, against all human possibilities. Insofar as this Feast of the Holy Family, begun at the urging of Pope John XXIII, is meant to call families to a deeper common life, this text ought to make clear that the key element in such common life is dependence on grace, on the surprising and merciful action of God.

The Second Lesson (Colossians 3:12-17), in Lutheran use, gathers the community around the mystery of Christmas. The community that sings spiritual songs—like the song of Simeon, inspired by the Spirit—is gathered around the Word of Christ, dwelling richly among us—like the one who is present as light in the Word and Sacrament in our midst. As that community, we are then enabled to give thanks to God the Father through Christ—like Anna singing out her praise beside the present child—and are clothed with the habit of Christmas: compassion, kindness, forgiveness, love. This deutero-Pauline image of the worshiping church assembly may become a symbol of the present congregation around the Christmas Gospel.

The Episcopal and Common lectionaries read, instead, the genuine Pauline passage, *Gal. 4:4-7,* primarily for its phrase "born of a woman." By this actual human birth the community is made heirs of freedom.

The Roman lectionary chooses *Heb. 11:8, 11-12, 17-19,* in which Abraham, Sarah, and Isaac again appear. This reading serves to underscore the sense of promise and grace present in the Roman First Lesson, by speaking of the gift to a woman "when she was past the age" and a man when "he was as good as dead" (Heb. 11:11-12). Abraham and Sarah, like the aged Anna and the dying Simeon of the Gospel, see the concrete mercy of God in a child. This reading, if its indications are followed, helps widen the Roman readings beyond the theme of the family toward the theme of grace, the mercy by which all people, including those who live in families, may be refreshed and restored to hope and life.

AROUND THE TEXTS

The First Sunday after Christmas may occur in the midst of or very near to the three ancient saint's days that follow Christmas: St. Stephen, the first martyr (December 26); St. John, the evangelist (December 27); and the Holy Innocents, the children slain in Bethlehem according to Matt. 2:13-18 (December 28). Although the origin of the first two of these days may have preceded the widespread acceptance of December 25 as the feast of Christ's nativity, the sequence of three days has come to be interpreted as an unfolding of the meaning of Christmas. Bernard of Clairvaux proposed that each of the commemorated people brought martyrdom, in deed or will, as their homage to the newborn child. Durandus, the thirteenth-century commentator on the liturgy, called them all the *comites Christi,* the "companions of Christ." T. S. Eliot, in his play *Murder in the Cathedral,* has Thomas Becket preach about them as witnesses to the union of nativity and cross, of rejoicing and mourning, in the mystery of Christ at Christmas.

We may continue in this tradition. *Stephen* sees Christ in the heavens, reminding us again of the liturgy's understanding of Christ as the sun (Acts 7:55-56). But he makes witness to what he sees with his life, in a death patterned after the Lukan story of Jesus' own death, handing over his spirit and begging mercy for his enemies (Acts 7:59-60; cf. Luke 23:34, 46). Christ has come in the flesh, light to be seen in the world, but Stephen's death shows the opposition to that light and points to Christ's own sufferings. *John,* the evangelist of the principal Gospel of Christmas, bears further witness to the light that is seen in the world. "That . . . which we have heard, which we have seen with our eyes, which we have looked upon and touched with our hands, concerning the word of life" (1 John 1:1) is the very presence of Christ, the central meaning of the Christian transformation of solstice. *The Holy Innocents* bear further witness to the sufferings of the one who has come. Herod is seeking to kill Jesus (Matt. 2:8, 12). With the birth of Christ in the world, rulers and kings are afraid. The governmental murder of the children (and all unjust sufferings everywhere, not just Christian martyrdoms, for the children of Bethlehem are hardly Christians) is seen as prefiguring the sufferings of Christ. The Word of God incarnate in the world shares the lot of the wretched ones of the earth, being with them as a down payment on God's justice. The riches of God's mercy and presence, the true solstice riches, are for those outside of the human distribution of justice and peace.

"The companions of Christ" join with Simeon and Anna, giving emphasis to the very themes that are important in today's Gospel: light, suffering, and a community that bears witness to both.

The Name of Jesus (January 1)

Lutheran	Roman Catholic	Episcopal	Common Lectionary
Num. 6:22-27	Num. 6:22-27	Exod. 34:1-8	Num. 6:22-27
Rom. 1:1-7 *or* Phil. 2:9-13	Gal. 4:4-7	Rom. 1:1-7	Gal. 4:4-7 *or* Phil. 2:9-13
Luke 2:21	Luke 2:16-21	Luke 2:15-21	Luke 2:15-21

ABOUT THE TEXTS

The Gospel (Luke 2:21) for this day in the Lutheran lectionary is the verse in Luke that tells of the naming of Jesus. This single verse is the second of three passages that Luke begins with the phrase "the days were fulfilled" (*eplēsthēsan hēmerai*). The same words are also used at the birth (2:6) and at the presentation (2:22), and they are often translated as "the time came." With these words Luke marks off a nativity triptych, and our simple verse functions as the second scene in showing forth the birth, naming, and presentation of Jesus.

In this verse it is eight days that are fulfilled, the requisite number for circumcision (Lev. 12:3) and for naming (Luke 1:59). There is no indication in the text that the circumcision plays any symbolic significance in Luke's intention. The next story, the account of the presentation, will juxtapose Jesus to temple sacrifice (see above on the Gospel for the First Sunday after Christmas) and will present the obedience of his parents to the law. But here there is no mention of the law nor is there anything made of a "first bloodletting," a point of considerable interest in some medieval exegesis that regarded this text as a hidden symbol of the Passion.

Rather, the point of this part of the triptych is the naming. Here too, however, Luke's interest does not seem to be drawn to the etymological meaning of Jesus' name (as does Matthew's interest in the account of Joseph's dream [Matt. 1:21]), nor to the fact that Jesus' name represents in Greek the name Joshua, the name of the one who led the people into God's land. Instead, the text recalls the annunciation of the angel, pulling into present consideration, into the nativity triptych, everything that the angel said about Jesus' identity. Jesus' name is thus presented as a summary of the lively and irresistible word of God, the word that was in the mouth of the angel sent from God's presence (1:19, 26) and the word to which Mary assents, "Let it be to me according to your word." The angel begins the description of the office and titles of the Messiah with his name: Jesus (1:31). Because the angel has said so, the thing comes about. Nothing is said in 2:21 of the parents or the parents' decision. The name is word of God. In this text then, the name Jesus sums up the word and action of God.

Today is the octave of Christmas, an "after-feast" one week after the great day, meant to receive and echo the meaning of the feast itself. When read on this day, this Gospel is intended as more than an historical reenactment of the eight days until the circumcision. Rather, it uses the name of Jesus as the summary of the Word of God at Christmas. In that name the whole message of the angel and the entire gospel is present.

Today is also New Year's Day, the day in the secular calendar that popularly expresses much of the classic solstice sense of old things yielding to new. Words of greeting and new beginning, of resolution and of wishes for good fortune, are widely exchanged on this day. In a Christian assembly on New Year's Day a single word is made to respond to these purposes: a name. In biblical use, of course, a name carries within itself the whole reality and meaning—even the presence—of the person named. It is not simply that the content of the annunciation—Jesus' Davidic kingship and his titles—are recalled. With his name comes the whole gospel account of his ministry, passion, and resurrection. The assembly gathers in this name, in the reality of Jesus' presence, passion, and resurrection. "In his name" the assembly is associated with the ancient purposes of Israel: the proclamation of God's mercy in the world, the priestly service of God's people in the world. "In his name" the assembly baptizes, interprets Scripture, and is enabled to give praise and thanks to God. Such are the new beginnings and resolutions, the "new year," that ever mark the faith.

In the Roman, Episcopal, and Common lectionaries the reading of this verse is lengthened with the addition of v. 15 (or v. 16) to v. 20, the account of the visit of the shepherds and of Mary keeping "all these things, pondering them in her heart." The "things" (*ta hrēmata,* 2:19) that Mary keeps, like the Hebrew *devarim,* could also be called "words." It is a "word," a "thing," a *hrēma,* that Mary assents to (1:38), that the shepherds go to see (2:15), and that has been "told them concerning this child" (2:17). The word of God and the action of God are one. The name of Jesus is a "word" that sums up all the gospel, giving this assembly its new year identity. And the Solemnity of the Mother of God, as Roman use calls this octave of Christmas and New Year's Day, proposes Mary to us as a figure of the church receiving and keeping this word.

The First Lesson (Numbers 6:22-27) is the text of the Aaronic benediction. In the midst of a miscellany of laws of Priestly origin collected in Numbers there stands this little liturgical fragment, the words the priests use whenever they bless the people. The words of blessing, protection, peace, and grace

are all associated with the lifted face of the LORD. The image of the turned
face is drawn from court life: When the monarch looks "with favor" on
a petitioner or a courtier, that person's lot improves. But the connotations
here are much wider: The revealed face of the LORD is God's presence no
longer hidden. Such a "face" enables the encounter of Israel with God, a
meeting in grace and not in judgment.

Saying such liturgical words is called "putting my name upon the people"
(6:27). This is so because the name of God, the tetragrammaton YHWH
(translated traditionally and inaccurately as LORD), is itself present in the
text and the text is "put upon the people." But it is even more deeply so
because the name of God is the presence of God, the encounterability of
God. The name of God enables and includes that meeting of Israel with
God envisioned in the blessing. The name of God "upon the people" is
the same thing as the people encountering God's gracious face and living
in peace.

Read next to the Gospel of the day, this text underscores the biblical
meaning of the word "name." Even more, it brings to light the Christian
faith in which, in the encounter with the reality of Jesus, the present
community encounters the gracious face of God. There are no Aaronic
priests in the church who have a right, authorized by this law, to speak
this blessing. Christians believe that the assembly in the name of Jesus
gathers in the reality of this blessing, in the name of God put upon the
people. Some Christian traditions have dared to end their liturgies with
this blessing, *not* because they regard their officers as having such a right,
but because that end-position indicates that the biblical quotation is a
summary of the entire interaction of the liturgy. In the assembly, the Scripture reading, the preaching, the prayers, the table thanksgiving, the eating
and drinking—all of these "in Jesus' name"—the name and face of God
have been present with peace and grace.

When read in the midst of the twelve days of the Christmas feast, the
text calls the assembly to see in the encounterability of the man Jesus the
very shining face of God. In Advent we have prayed, "Let your face shine
on us, and we shall be saved" (Ps. 80:3). In Christmas we behold the
shining face.

The Episcopal lectionary reads *Exod. 34:1-8* as the First Lesson. The
intention is similar to that in the use of the Aaronic benediction. The LORD
passes before Moses who is hidden, alone, in the mountain and proclaims
the name of the LORD. The text calls our attention to the "name" and to
God's activity in the name. Read in the season of Christmas it invites us
all to see, in the face of Christ, what Moses saw alone.

The Second Lesson (Romans 1:1-7), in Lutheran and Episcopalian use,
explicitly gathers a church around this mystery of the name of Jesus. It is

the church at Rome that is addressed. By the reading of this text today, its meaning is extended to whatever assembly is the place of its reading. Paul speaks the gospel to that assembly, and the content of the gospel is Jesus Christ as Son of God, not by Davidic claim and royal meaning, but according to the Spirit active in the resurrection of the crucified. The content of the gospel is "his name among all the nations" (1:5). The present assembly is also called and gathered around that name. And so, just as in the priestly benediction, grace and peace are spoken to the assembly from God. This text enacts, at the beginning of Romans, what one hears at the end of 2 Corinthians and at the outset of many liturgies: "The grace of our Lord Jesus Christ, the love of God, and the communion of the Holy Spirit be with you all." The text calls the community into the triune life of God: The Spirit of the resurrection gathers us around the name of Jesus and so into God's grace.

Alternative Second Lessons for this day include *Phil. 2:9-13,* the end of the Christ-hymn in which all knees are envisioned as bending at the name of Jesus, and *Gal. 4:4-7,* in which Christ is proclaimed as "born of woman" (see above on the alternative Second Lesson for the First Sunday after Christmas). The latter reading is meant to accord with the intention of the Roman lectionary in giving the octave of Christmas a Marian theme.

AROUND THE TEXTS

Today is the octave of Christmas. Although the custom of observing octaves is not widely discussed in current worship, the pattern of the eighth day of the feast is deeply important for Christian liturgy. This custom may have been rooted in the eight days of the Jewish feast of tabernacles (John 7:37; Lev. 23:36), a feast that came to be filled with eschatological longing for the day of God. For Christians, the resurrection itself is the "eighth day," the new day of God, the day beyond what is possible in the recurring pattern of the seven-day planetary week. Each Sunday is the octave of the last Sunday, continuing the "eight days later" (John 20:26) of the disciples' meetings with the risen one. Each Sunday is a kind of octave of Easter. The feast of Easter is a great octave. It is made up of eight Sundays, the eighth Sunday being the feast of Pentecost. On this pattern, other great feasts in the calendar began to have their octaves in medieval liturgical practice, a practice that has widely disappeared. But January 1 remains as the octave of Christmas.

An octave echoes, proclaims, and intensifies the first day of the feast; therefore every Sunday proclaims the resurrection and gathers us around the Risen One. Pentecost pours into our hearts all the meaning of the great fifty-day Easter feast, enlivened by the Spirit of the resurrection. This day proclaims again the meaning of Christmas. It may do this by focusing the mystery of Christ's birth in the name of Jesus or by holding before us the idea of the "birth-giver of God." In either case, the feast is intended as a cup from which we may drink the wine of Christmas.

Secular calendar customs have made the first day of the new year to be the octave of the old date of the solstice. The sun begins to return, is safely under way, and we count a new year. Many of the ancient customs of the solstice have come to be especially associated with this day and with the evening that awaits its coming—role reversals and foolishness, processions and drunkenness. Some Christians use the evening for a watch-night, a modern day counterobservance for a modern-day Saturnalia. But whether or not Christians go to parties, this day dawns to proclaim another solstice content and another kind of new year—the mystery and increasing light of grace.

The Second Sunday after Christmas

Lutheran	Roman Catholic	Episcopal	Common Lectionary
Isa. 61:10—62:3	Sir. 24:1-2, 8-12	Jer. 31:7-14	Jer. 31:7-14 or Sir. 24:1-2, 8-12
Eph. 1:3-6, 15-18	Eph. 1:3-6, 15-18	Eph. 1:3-6, 15-19a	Eph. 1:3-6, 15-18
John 1:1-18	John 1:1-18	Matt. 2:13-15, 19-23	John 1:1-18

ABOUT THE TEXTS

The Gospel (John 1:1-18) that is read on those occasions when *two* Sundays fall in the twelve days between Christmas and Epiphany is a further repetition of the great Christmas text, the Johannine prologue (see above on the Gospel of the Christmas Service in the Day). Today this text is read with its full eighteen verses, so that Christmas is held out to us as the continued feast in which we receive overflowingly from Christ's fullness (1:16). As with the Episcopal alternative on the First Sunday after Christmas, this reading is repeated here partly for pedagogical reasons: Too many people may have not heard this text at Christmas, having heard only the Lukan nativity, thus missing the great proclamation of the church. But there is a sense in which this text is always appropriate. At each Sunday meeting of the assembly—and certainly in all the days of Christmas—the church proclaims the incarnate Word of God, the full glory of God, mercifully present in its midst.

The Episcopal alternative for this Sunday (*Matt. 2:13-15, 19-23*) is the account of the flight into Egypt. Here the story of the child being called out of Egypt suggests that in Jesus the history of the exodus is being recapitulated. Jesus is the new Israel. Like the ancient people, he is brought out of Egypt for the purposes of God. The threat to the child, made even stronger in the passage omitted, the slaughter of the innocents (2:16-18), suggests ahead of time the strength of the opposition to those purposes, foreshadowing the passion of Christ.

In Matthew 2—as in the "knew him not . . . received him not" of John 1 or the "sign that is spoken against" of Luke 2—a connection is made to the cross. Each of the Gospel readings of Christmas push us toward the paschal mystery: It is in the death and resurrection of Christ that we meet all that these texts say that he is. Christmas is not just the story of a baby. Each of the gatherings around the Christmas Gospel is also a gathering to remember his death at a meal and to encounter his resurrection in the signs of his body and blood.

The First Lesson (Isaiah 61:10—62:3) of the Lutheran lectionary also repeats an earlier reading. This exultant text from Third Isaiah is the choice of the Episcopal and Common lectionaries for the First Sunday after Christmas and has already been read in part by the other lectionaries on the Third Sunday in Advent, the old Sunday of rejoicing. Here the rejoicing expected in Advent has become the rejoicing present in Christmas. In Third Isaiah, the city is clothed as if for a wedding and the city's salvation has become a bright light before the world. In Christmas, the world is clothed with mercy, and the salvation of the wretched little ones of the earth already begins to show its light as God in Christ lies down with the poor.

The First Lesson in the Roman lectionary (*Sir. 24:1-2, 8-12*), which is also an alternative reading in the Common Lectionary, is a hymn about Lady Wisdom. The great Wisdom of God, through whom God created the world, by which God knows and upholds all things, came to be personified as *hokmah, sophia,* Lady Wisdom, in much of the poetry of the wisdom tradition (cf. Prov. 9:1-6). Here, she is commanded to make her tent and dwelling place in Israel. Israel will know her in the presence of the word and the law in the midst of the people (cf. Psalm 147, the psalm of the day). This common theme in the later wisdom literature is important background to the hymn about the Word in John 1. Read here, next to the prologue of John, it serves to underscore that background. It is the very Wisdom of God, known and beloved in Israel, that has tented among us in Christ (John 1:14) and is known as overflowing grace.

The Episcopal and Common lectionaries choose *Jer. 31:7-14,* a splendid passage promising concrete consolations to returning exiles: "with weeping they shall come . . . with consolations I will lead them back" (31:9). The text forms another of the biblical texts that depicts the return of exiles as a new exodus. Read next to the account of the flight into Egypt, the child and the mother are seen to be among the returning throng (31:8). Thus the sufferings of Christ are seen to be among these exiles—and through them, among all the wretched of the earth. And the little return from Egypt is made an image of the resurrection, of the comfort of God for all these people. Already now, in this assembly at the Eucharist, we begin to eat of "the grain, the wine, and the oil" (31:12) that God means to set before the hungry of the world. Christmas is then seen as a down payment on God's intention.

The Second Lesson (Ephesians 1:3-6, 15-18) is part of the rhetorically rich and complex beginning of the deutero-Pauline Letter to the Ephesians. Such a rich text belongs in Christmas, imaging in its very wealth, like a Christmas pudding, all that there is in Christ. When it is read as an image of the present congregation gathered around the texts of the day, we may hear the text thus: You are in Christ, chosen in Christ, graced in Christ. He is at the center of this gathering. May you then have wisdom—the very Wisdom that tents among us in the incarnation. And may you see God's light, the light that is shown forth, throughout this Christian solstice, in the darkness of a world that longs to know God. And may you be renewed in hope for the world itself, for all the poor who need such a return from exile and such a reception of overflowing grace as the texts of Christmas describe.

AROUND THE TEXTS

The feast of Christmas is twelve days long. This is reflected in the popularity of the secular gift-giving carol: "On the first day of Christmas." We need to learn it in the church. If Advent in the assembly can be marked by simplicity and waiting, even while celebration is already going on in stores or in other places in our own lives, then Christmas can be a full twelve-day feast, even when the culture stops the celebration at New Year's Day. The clock of the assembly ought to be slightly off in relationship to the clock of the world. Christmas is about the reception but also the transformation of the world's feast.

Simple concrete practices can be images for this transformation. The tree can stay up for the twelve days, to be taken down and burned on twelfth night, January 5. The burning, yet another symbol of the light against the darkness, might be at the center of a parish party. Pageants and *posadas* can be held throughout the twelve days, retelling the nativity story then, rather than during Advent, a time that is already too harried. Gifts and food can be given to the homeless and to relief agencies, especially as these gifts represent a deeper commitment from the parish to engage in such witness to the incarnation throughout the new year. And Christmas carols and hymns in all their richness can be sung at gatherings in the church all through the twelve days.

When a Sunday occurs in the midst of the twelve days, it becomes an especially important occasion to continue the richness of the twelve-day feast. Now the meaning of Sunday—the gathering of the assembly in the risen Christ before the face of God—is seen in the light of the Christmas mystery: The incarnate Word is at the center of the gathering and the song of angels is on our lips. And the community is renewed to give witness in the world to an ever-present feast that is meant for all people, to the fullness of grace in Christ, from which we all receive (John 1:16).

It is hard to believe in such grace in our day. It is easier to stop the feast quickly, guiltily. But is there really abundant grace for the poor, for the religion-bound, for the aching world? Has a sun dawned that will really give light? The crucified Christ, God come to lie down with the poor, is the presence in the world of much greater abundance than solstice festivities ever imagined. Throughout this feast the word in our ears, the life-giving meal in our mouths, and the new song to God on our lips invite us to believe it is so.